THE LIE THAT MADE ME

MARK TUGWELL

LONDON'S finest

London's Finest Distribution
London, UK

London's Finest Distribution

First published in Great Britain in 2018
by LONDON'S FINEST DISTRIBUTION

www.LondonFinestDistribution.com
Info@londonsfinestdistribution.com
IG: Londons_Authors_United

Disclaimer
This is a work of creative nonfiction. The events are portrayed to the best of my memory. While all the stories in this book are true, some names and identifying details have been changed to protect the privacy of the people involved.

ISBN 978-0-9935900-3-0
Printed and bound by CPI Group (UK) Ltd, Croydon CR0 4YY

This book is written in Jamaican and English street language idiom.

The Lie That Made Me

Mark Tugwell

PRAISE FOR

The Lie That Made Me

Mark Tugwell

"Mark Tugwell's 'The Lie That Made Me' is one of hope, in the face of much adversity. This book is a must read for all who think that crime pays. It is a sign of the times and a look into the future, for all who think that jail is some sort of joke. A very serious insight, from a ex-career criminal with a total of 23 years behind bars to show for it. There is nothing pleasant about this book, but a much needed wake up call to all you would be criminals. Very interesting!" - *Chris Sibia: Author*

AUTHOR'S ACKNOWLEDGEMENTS

First of all I would like to give a huge thanks to the Almighty. Mum and Dad I love you both, my one son Owen and two daughters, Candice and Chelsea. Thank you Adrian Dixon aka Blacks who introduced me to Chris Sibia, the man who helped me write this book. I would like to also give a big shout out to all the people who have always been there for me and to my brothers, Andrew and Christopher and sister Evonne. Mark Mills, Diane Caan and Paul Mittoo big up yourselves and RIP to all my people who have passed away.

PROLOGUE

Crack House

Chapter 1

I had a problem now all my food (crack) was done! The crackhead I was with said, 'Come do this job with me, we go 50/50 on whatever I get.' *He was a professional storage unit thief.* I was cool with that, being prang (high) from the crack, paranoid and not functioning at my best, I wasn't trying to do anything other than smoke, *being a lookout was light work.*

So he went and did it, 10 minutes max he was in and out. As we were making our get away, we saw some scaffolders working on a house on Capworth Street, Leyton, East London. The stuff we had was perfect for their trade, so this guy gets out to go talk to them about the stolen goods. *They must have looked at him and thought, what a crackhead cos I would have if I was them.* That's probably why they only offered him £150. The goods were worth at least £600, but all we cared about was smoking more crack.

When he came back and asked me if he should take the £150, I told him, 'Take that! If we need to do another job when the crack's finished, we just touch road and do another job, simple!' He agreed and took the £150. As we drove back to the crack house he gave me £25 and told me, 'I'll give you the rest later.' I should have told him I wanted it all now, but true I was weak, I said, 'cool' because it was enough for one crack rock.

But when I finished piping that rock, I wanted more and this guy was in the bathroom with his whore, fucking her and getting high. I asked the local drug dealer,

'Yo, how much did he buy?'

He said, '£125 worth.' *Taking me for a dickhead, yeah!* I banged on the door, for what felt like 20 minutes, half an hour and this guy's not answering. *It's like he didn't know I will turn over this whole yard.*

I decide to leave it for now because I was on edge, and wasn't at my best. He didn't know I was a terrorist yet. In his eyes I just liked to smoke crack, but I was going to have to educate him now for this, furthermore all of them.

Over the next few days, I went to the crack house as normal. But after that disrespect and the paranoia that comes with piping crack every day, with people who can't be trusted, I decided I wasn't sharing my crack with any of them. I would ask them though. 'Yo, you want some of my ting?' *Crack heads never said no to crack,* so I would set up the pipe, then as they reached, I would draw it back and pipe it myself, blowing the smoke out in their face. That pissed them off, but as they looked in my eyes, they could see I was too serious for them.

I was begging anyone of them would move to me, so I could violate and feel like I was defending myself. I was having trouble controlling the anger that was building every day I thought about it, but they didn't want anything with the new face I was showing them.

The day finally came where I couldn't wait anymore. I was still teasing them, and they still weren't taking the bait. I had smoked off all my ting and was looking to leave the yard to go make some more money, so I could buy more crack. But as I got to the front door, music was playing in the kitchen. I looked in and saw one of my bredrins spitting bars like him name big MC. I looked behind him and saw that same pussy that had bumped (robbed) me giggling. I knew he wasn't, but I acted like he was giggling at me. I walked into the kitchen and picked up a tray that he was standing next to on the counter. It had "white heroin" on it. I asked, 'You see this, is it yours?'

He said, 'Yeah.'

I said, 'GOOD,' and threw it on the floor, then stamped it into the ground. *Someone on heroin needed it, so it had to be on now!* 'You want to smile and laugh like I'm a joke yeah, laugh now!' I said. His eyes widened with shock as he rushed me, pushing me up against the wall screaming,

'WHAT THE FUCK DO YOU THINK YOU'RE DOING?' He didn't know how glad I was he did that. I took out my borer and poked him once in his belly, as I took control of the situation "I-mmediately".

I told him, 'YOU DON'T SEE, TODAY I MIGHT KILL YOU IN THIS BLOODCLART.' I went straight to auto pilot as I quickly got him where I wanted. My borer (knife) ready to poke him again! All the onlockers frozen and shook to death (scared) watching in silence.

I said, 'PUSSY, MOVE AGAIN!' He struggled a little cos the first poke must have hurt. I poked him again. 'LISTEN ME PUSSY, KNOW WHO YOU FUCKING WID NEXT TIME YOU WHAN FUCK,' and poked him again. 'TAKE BAD MAN FOR FOOL, YEAH?' poked him again. 'I FEEL TO KILL YOU IN HERE TODAY PUSSY,' poked him again. He froze and went limp, with a faint murmur begging me not to kill him. Blood was leaking everywhere, as he got ready to bleed out and believe me, I had the whole house in check. It's only then he realised ah killer he did fuck wid. The drug dealers heard the commotion and came to see what was going on.

These yardie dealers started begging me, 'PLEASE YANKEE, just leave the yard now.'

'I'LL LEAVE THIS BLOODCLART WHEN I'M READY, furthermore get the big man on the phone now and tell him I want some food (crack) and I'm not paying for it.' *Bout they come from South, trying to run shit on my ends!* Big man gave me what I wanted, then I left the yard. *My wings had grown back.* After that they called me "The Scary Movie" and I could do what I wanted to in there now.

Message for Future Generations

Before I tell you what happened next, let me start from the beginning because I wasn't always like that. I am a product of my environment and the reality is, I can only blame myself for the life I lived. I was given many chances to change, but I didn't see anything wrong with the way I was living. I wanted to be a bad boy. I didn't see a problem with drugs. I didn't think about the many victims of the many crimes I committed, or the ripple effect I was having on my community. I wanted to be remembered as a G, but the harsh reality is, when you get locked up, life goes on and no one cares. The world quickly forgets you. Your partner leaves you. If you have children they learn to live without you and they might lose all respect for you. It took a total of 23 years behind bars for me to see this. It took living alongside lifers to realise my life is worth more than that and I, like all of us, have the ability to change. This is me giving something back to my community; trying to make sure some of the next generation learn from the many mistakes I made. I want to deter as many people as possible from following in my footsteps.

Jail is a waste of life, modern day slavery and let's be clear, they do not want rehabilitation. They have made the prison system into a business that makes them a lot of money. The prison system loves re-offenders, so let my story be a lesson to all of you. If you let them get you like they got me, they will have you for life. My IPP (Imprisoned for Public Protection) finishes when I'm 134 years old, which means probation will see me whenever they like for the rest of my life. I can't leave the country unless they allow me to and my children, how can I ever make this up to them?

This is my story!

Flatbush 1971

I was born in London, England 1966, but moved to Flatbush, Brooklyn with my "Mum" and Dad when I was 4. A few months after we got there, my "Mum's" work friend Shirley who had lived in England too, came to live with us. We thought Shirley came to the States for a better life like we had, but she really had another motive. She stayed with us while she worked, and saved until she had enough money to get her own place.

After about six months, she had made enough. So my Dad offered to help her move and for some reason decided to take me. *In hindsight I wish he hadn't!* The yard (house) was a basic one bedroom, but it was clean, so it could work. After we had helped her unpack, Dad told me 'wait here' and left me in the front room.

'Yes Daddy,' I told him as he left me on the sofa with nothing to do but patiently wait, wondering what he was doing. True it was day time, I could hear things going on outside which distracted me for a while, but as time passed and Dad still hadn't come back, the little boy curiosity got the better of me. I opened the front room door and heard funny noises coming from the bedroom. I wondered what that was, so I went and looked cos the door was open and that's when I saw Dad. He was fucking my "Mum's" and his Wife's "friend" Shirley on her new bed.

Apparently they had been fucking while my "Mum" had been at work since she got to America, but this information was on a need to know basis and at that age, I just didn't need to know. *At the time I didn't know exactly what they were doing, but I knew that kind of togetherness was supposed to be with my "Mum", not her "friend".* But Dad was my Super Hero, he knew best, so I went and sat my little ass down and waited for him like nothing happened. When they finished, he came out and told me 'Just say we helped Shirley move her stuff, ok?' Basically *"Don't fuck up my shit!"* When we got back home, I went along with everything he said so it was cool and from that day, Dad would go meet Shirley whenever he liked because now she had her own place.

That year I remember me and my Mum going to Jamaica for the first time during the summer holidays. We left Dad in Brooklyn keeping up fuckery with Shirley the witch, which was her new name, while Mum took me on tour. I didn't know her old stomping ground, Tivoli Gardens was so serious and the man dem on that block would influence so much of my future.

I was 5 years old at the time and all I remembered was the hustle and bustle of Carnation Gardens Fish Market. *I had a lovely time in the sun with my "Mum."*

When the holiday ended, I went back to Brooklyn and got back to life with Dad and the witch doing their ting secretly and getting away with it all though 1971 into 1972. My Dad was doing well, so he had plenty of disposable income. Life was good, other than him regularly cheating on "Mum."

In the summer of 1972, Dad decided to take me back to Jamaica with him and show me Jamaica from his point of view. I can remember that trip more, because I was a little older and he took me to my Grand Mum's house, where I met both of my Grand Parents and my Dad's siblings. I remember one of my Aunts had a church, but we didn't go to it because my Dad wasn't religious. It was another lovely summer holiday memory, but all good things came to an end and it seemed like I blinked twice and it was time to go home, back to Brooklyn.

When we got home, my Dad continued his affair clean into 1973 without getting caught. However in 1973 my "Mum" found out. I don't know how, but she did so they began arguing about it and from time to time, my Dad would beat her up on a wrong and strong ting. Then he would leave the house and we wouldn't see him again for days, leaving me with "Mum." This woman Shirley and my Dad's relationship started affecting me from then and I could see it because my Super Hero was missing. I spent hours crying and waiting by the door for him every day he stayed out. I loved him so much, I would have done anything he told me to, including kill.

Anytime he invited me to come, I was on it, but at the same time, I knew I was betraying "Mum" being around that witch, so I would rebel in her honour. When my Dad tried to force me to be nice, I wouldn't listen and the only time I was nice to her was when I felt like it. She wasn't nice to me, so being nice to her was long. *Hatred for her was growing daily from then.*

I'm 7 years old now and I've started going school in Brooklyn, down the road from where we live. I'm an angry little boy, but at home I'm just a boy. I have no one I can take my anger out on. *I needed to release these feelings on someone.*

Being new and from England, some of the boys in my class didn't like me, so it didn't take long before they were trying to punk me off. There were too many of them to fight all at the same time, so they took the piss for a while, but it wasn't in my nature to have that shit, so before long I decided to fight back and went for the main one.

He always used to tell me, 'After school I'm gonna beat your ass.'

So I told him, 'Today we'll see who gets their ass beat' and just like that the scene was set. Everyone was outside ready to watch that fight when school finished. The guy was just expecting to casually beat me up in front of all them people, but as he went to take off his jacket, I did rass him with a lick (hit him hard). His jacket tangled him up and I knew that if I wanted to win the fight, this was the time. I managed to twist him up then drop him. When he landed on the floor, I sat on his chest and squeezed his neck until I saw his face turning red. Everyone stopped it after that and I had won the fight. Now he knew I wasn't a punk, him and his boys decided to be my friends.

Now I'm in with the popular yutes, I would roll with them and get involved when they were stealing from sweet shops and bunking off school (cutting class). We were all good yutes really, just getting into a little trouble here and there. But after I got that first bad school report and my "Mum" came down and beat me in front of everyone, including the teachers. I was fighting constantly after that because every day a different yute would bring it up laughing, saying 'He got beat up by his "Mum", he can't fight no one.' That was a massive disrespect that I couldn't have, so any one talking that shit had to get it. Due to that I got known for getting into trouble and it started becoming the norm.

In school day to day when we weren't bunking, or getting into shit, we spent most of our time in the same class with the same teacher, teaching us everything. I did like going to that school. All the girls were feeling me cos of my English accent and I enjoyed the attention I got from most of them. There were a few girls I wasn't trying to fuck with though. The big burly bitches that would try beat up boys. *I had to fight them like I was fighting man certain times, they were so tough.* I guess you could say it was all part of the Brooklyn experience because Brooklyn was rough, so me and my friends took practice fighting serious. We had to, and sparring became our favourite pastime. We were getting ready for what we subconsciously knew was coming. (*A Hard Knock Life*).

At lunchtime, because I only lived a few blocks away, I would go home for lunch and eat proper food. The canteen food was alright, but "Mum" was a spectacular cook and she used to bring things from work too because she was a nurse.

After school I would do my homework, then I was allowed to play out til my Dad got home. As soon as he got in, I would run and jump on him. Both legs wrapped around him and from then, for the rest of the evening it was all about my Dad. That's if he didn't leave me to go spend time with the witch Shirley. Sometimes he took me to her house, but it wasn't the same as when he was home and he would make me lie to "Mum" and tell her we went to link his bredrins, instead of telling her the truth.

This is where I began to see the sense in lying because as time went on, if he told the truth they argued, so I began to wish he would just lie because I didn't like to hear their constant arguing. She knew he was still fucking the witch and that was obviously a problem.

"Aunt" Cherry

Chapter 2

Things got so bad, my Dad decided he was sending me back to London for a while to see my "Aunt" Cherry while he sorted it out. Some of his friends were flying to England around the time, so he made me fly with them on a little 2 week vacation. *It was the summer of 1975*. I had just turned 9 years old and I remember walking through customs and seeing my "Aunt" standing there waiting for me. When she saw me, the hug she gave me was massive, it was like a Mum type hug. On the way home, she couldn't stop looking at me. I didn't think anything of it, but I noticed. When we got to her house and I unpacked, that's when she called me downstairs.

'Mark, I need to tell you something.' There was a pause as she looked at me, then she said, 'You know I'm really your Mum, don't you?'

'WHAT, I thought you was my Aunt and Andrew was my cousin.'

'No, that's not true, you don't see the resemblance? It was supposed to be a secret because your Dad is playing happy families with his wife. But I just can't keep it in anymore because you need to know the truth.'

'So, you mean to tell me, all these years you made me think you was my Aunt?' I said.

'Mark, your Dad was married and back then what we did was

taboo, your Dad asked me to have a baby for him and his wife. Your Grandma, my Mum, gave me hell and disowned me because of you. Your Dad was the provider and he didn't want any extra trouble with his wife, so it was just easier to leave you with him.'

Now she was telling me this, shit started to make sense. It was a little hard to take in as a 9 year old and what could I say. I had to go with the flow for now, until I got back to Brooklyn. But when I got back, I asked my Dad straight. I needed him to tell me, *Your Aunt's crazy and she's lying,* but he confirmed she was telling the truth.

'Mark, let me tell you how it went' he said to me. 'Way before you were born, I was admitted into Hospital because something was wrong with my appendix. I met your Mum, Madge and Shirley who were all nurses in the same Hospital at the time. Madge ended up looking after me and I fell in love with her. I couldn't resist a good-looking woman and your Mum and Shirley loved me off too, I was spoilt for choice. Do you understand what I'm telling you Mark?'

'Yes Dad', I said listening carefully.

'Me and Madge started seeing each other when I got out of hospital and that's when she told me she couldn't have children, but I wanted at least one. So, we talked about it and decided to ask your Mum if she would be our surrogate and your Mum agreed.

'Why didn't you tell me though Dad?' I asked.

'We thought it would be best if we didn't, Madge treated you well, didn't she?'

'Yes Dad, but you should have told me she wasn't really my Mum.'

My Dad kissed his teeth and told me, 'well I didn't and you know now, but make sure you keep it to yourself because everyone round here thinks Madge is your real Mum, and we are going to keep it like that, you hear me Mark?' *The Lie That Made Me started right here.*

The world as I knew it fell to pieces. My Dad went on to say, 'Your Mum was crazy anyway, she left you in the house as a baby and turned on the gas, like she was trying to kill you. The best thing I ever did was take you from her.'

I was in shock when he told me that, my Dad was trying to make me think I was better off not knowing my real Mum. *I didn't know what to believe*, but I was with my Dad, so I had to listen to what he was saying at least, even though I didn't want to believe my Mum would do something like that to me.

I thought about my new little brother in England that I wasn't growing up with and my "Mum" who I knew as Mum was really my Step Mum. She was a good woman and she had always treated me like her son, so it was always going to be love with her, but I had a whole new family now and on the flip side, none of Madge's family were really my blood. *My real family was all the way in England.* I just left my real Mum and I didn't know when I was gonna see her again. *It was only my Dad that was real family here.*

Now I knew this my attitude changed. My Dad had betrayed me big time. He was still my Super Hero but I had to wonder, could I really trust him? My real Mum had made a mess telling me the truth and I could tell my Dad was pissed with her, even though it needed to come out sooner rather than later. But at the same time it confused me as a yute. Madge was my "Mum" in my mind and when I was in Brooklyn, I would call her "Mum" and refer to my real Mum as Cherry. It was only the witch I had problems with because my Dad was still comfortably cheating on my "Mum" with her.

In school after that revelation I found it hard. I had one little Jamaican bredrin I clinged to called Sirfield, and some twins that knew a little martial arts and taught me how to back flip. But other than them guys, the only thing that kept me calm was sports. I was athletic and I would play with yutes all age groups and I was never out played regardless what we were playing. You could say being sporty ran in my family. *But school really became long and my Dad spent more and more time away.* I complained to him about all the time he spent with her and the fact he always left me.

This must have made my Dad feel guilty because he had actually married her on a sly and decided to tell me just then in the heat of the moment. *I was so hurt.*

I asked him, 'Dad, how could you marry her and not even tell me?'

He said, 'I didn't tell you because I couldn't trust you Mark!' Those words cut me deep, after everything he had done; he couldn't trust ME, WOW!

On top of that, now he was married to her, he really expected me to be nice and she would go out of her way to tell him and enjoy the licks he gave me, if I wasn't nice to her. My Dad was just hurting my feelings all over the place and he noticed a little change in me, so he decided to try including me in some of the things they were doing more often. It was too little too late though really, but I do remember him taking me to one birthday party I enjoyed around that time.

He wanted me and the witch to bond or something, but that wasn't going to happen. Not now, no way! I just wanted to have that relationship with my Dad because I still loved him. This party they took me to, was one of the witch's work colleagues twin daughter's, birthday party. I didn't want to go with the witch, but it was Daddy time, so I just went with it. When we got there and I met the twins I actually liked them, so we clicked straight away. *They both fancied me, and I liked the both of them too.*

During the day in play we ended up underneath the dining table, where the adults couldn't see what was going on playing, Doctor and Nurses; feel up feel up. That was a good day spent with my Dad and as I was getting older, I wasn't having many, so I held the good days close to me.

Back at school, I was going through the motions, but I wasn't really feeling it so I couldn't concentrate. The teachers were pissing me off, telling me shit they knew nothing about til one day I snapped. *Teachers always talk shit not thinking about how their words might affect you. Or maybe they know exactly what they're doing.* I didn't think about the consequences at the time which was, I was getting left behind. All I thought was he got what he deserved and I didn't care because I was already booked and counting down the days to my summer holiday. My Dad had booked for us to go back to Jamaica and I was looking forward to that.

The beginning of July just before my birthday we jumped on a plane going back to Montego Bay. My uncle was a hill and gully rider who took tourists all over the Island to make his money. When we arrived he was there as we went through customs, waiting for us. But surprise, surprise, as soon as we landed, my Dad was off doing his ting. He was a Jamaican with American engineer money, so in Jamaica he was classed as a Don. He had a lot to do and that didn't include me. On top of that, after about a week he decided to bounce and leave me there with my uncle, as punishment for getting left back in school. I knew he wasn't happy about that, but I was pissed. How could he just leave me with family I didn't even know like that? He even left me to wonder if I was going to have to stay in Jamaica and go to school there too. *I only had one bredrin there named Purnel.* We were the same age, so it was cool rolling with him, but I was beginning to dislike my Dad for playing these games with me. He would phone the family home and when I knew it was him, I would rush to the phone.

'Dad, I'll be good, just send me my return ticket please' I'd tell him.

He would ask, 'Are you sure you're going to be good Mark?' I wanted to go home so bad, I'd have said anything, but he dragged it out. Each week he would holla and each week I would say the same thing, until after 6 weeks he sent me my return ticket. *I got back to the Brooklyn resentful.* As a yute you pick up everything in your environment quickly, so I turned into a Yard yute. I had got to Jamaica dancing like an American and all the Jamaican's had laughed at me, but by the time I had got back to America, I was dancing like a Yard yute and my Dad was calling me names. *I thought, even at that age, well what do you expect Dad if you just leave me there?*

1978

We were living in flats up until now, but my "Mum" decided we needed to move into a house with more space. I was settled, and I didn't really want to move, but I was a yute who had to be seen and not heard. We were moving from the 40's to the 90's, East 94th Street and I was leaving Public School, where I had my school friends, to go to Meyer 11 Junior High.

I knew when we moved there I was never going to see these friends again and that was emotional. I was 12 turning 13 and I thought as I'm here in this new school on my own, it's better to be cool. But while I was out there trying to be nice, everyone else was out here telling me to wait til after school. 'Your ass is grass!' One of the guys in my class, Kendrick even told his friend a few years older than us, to come and violate me too. That afternoon as I left school, the first day, this guy came and started roughing me up.

I was telling him, 'Chill, chill!'

But he told me, 'If you don't fight back, this is going to happen until June.' *He left me that thought to marinate.* From September to June! That wasn't something I could work with, so the next day, I told Kendrick, 'Tell your boy, come.' I decided right there that we were gonna fight. The yute gladly accepted my challenge and he was there waiting for me at the back entrance, when I came out of school. I remember it was rainy and not the best conditions for fighting, but as soon as I got to him it was on. I Sugar Ray'd him! For every 1 lick he gave me, I gave him 5 until he gave up. It didn't take long and by the time I finished with him, he had a print of my knuckle in the top of his head. After that, the same guy who sent him to fight me wanted to talk to me, so we became friends. I thought that would have made me nice in the school, but boy was I wrong. Normally that would have, but I was in the baddest class in a bad school, so everybody was bad. I was put in that class because of the incident in my last school where I had snapped.

The teacher had told me, 'Don't make me have to tell your "Mum",' having heard about the time my step Mum came and beat me in front of everyone. But because of everything, I wasn't in the mood to hear this guy talking about my "Mum" because he didn't know shit about her, so I had attacked him with a chair. I know I shouldn't have done that, but he shouldn't have said what he said either. *But now it was me being punished with the degenerate class.*

It was a bit of a culture shock to me, but I was getting used to rolling with the punches. The down side to this that I didn't know was, I was put in the class with all the yutes that were expected to fail, leaving me with not much chance of passing. Or that might have been the plan, to get all the black children into the under performing class, so we would all fall behind and leave school with no qualifications, so our choices in life would be shit.

Once again, I'm starting afresh with no friends, having to make friends in Brooklyn, the Brooklyn way. Fight then be friends. *Punk never had no friend in Brooklyn.*

These yutes I was coming up with had parents on food stamps, or were ex war veterans who had turned junky from Brown (heroine) and were now bums, or both. *I was growing up with unruly yutes.* I was in a fight at least once a week and on top of that, we were at the beginning of what the world would call "Gang Culture".

I was one of the youngest in the gang on my block and every day I got back from school, the elders would take turns practicing their moves on me. This was when guys were getting knocked out and like now, the ego was real. I had to master my defence from early true that. *I came like Mayweather*. Life wouldn't be worth living in school if you got knocked out and some guys had started bringing in weapons because they couldn't fight. Mainly knives, but sometimes guns to make sure no one fucked around. You could say it was tense and not the best place to learn. If you add some young up and coming prostitutes to the mix, my school was the breeding ground for what we see today.

Within about a month, I had a new crew. There were 5 of us who were rolling and all we would do whenever we got a chance was spare with each other and look for fights with other crews cos we were ready for that.

I'm 13 all now and finding my feet nicely. Drugs came into the mix now, because my elders were operating from our local grocery store. It was like you see in the movies, with the hatch at the back. Man would knock and it would open up. A serious face would look and ask what drugs you wanted and how much. He would take the money then shut it back, go get the drugs then hand it out through the same hatch. This is where my elders got their big bits from, to hit the road selling and that's where I started to see things because my elder drug dealer bredrins would send me to do drop offs, or use me as a lookout.

This grocery shop was on our block and we were the town house yutes or Island Boys. Our parents had the big cars and on the outside, our lives looked nice. We were different to the local yutes down the road, who would sell drugs in their projects. No one really wanted to go into the projects to get their drugs, so we were doing better business. This made the Project Yutes come out talking about, 'this is our block' trying to take it over. That was obviously beef because that would have taken food out of our mouths. I was watching this as a runner, interested to see what was gonna happen next because some of them Project Yutes were serious, but so were us town house yutes and we had a lot to lose. We had cars pulling up all day, about 10 hands serving up the drugs, trying to make the sale. The guys in the cars would look for who he knew and buy from them, then the car would speed off. Man dem weren't just gonna let the Project Yutes come and take that over. CRAZY!

Around the time my Dad invited one of our family members from Northampton in England to visit us. He was my Dad's cousin, but he was the same age as me, so from he landed we were rolling and I was showing him wha gwan in Brooklyn. His name was Gary and it was good times when he was around because my Dad was cool. He was a good actor, but to be fair, when he was in a good mood he was generous and alright. That was the Dad I loved, he just wasn't that guy very often.

Gary stayed for the Summer Holiday as I ran for my elders and watched them do their ting, then when the holidays finished he went back home to Northampton. When he left, things went back to normal with my Dad and I continued watching what was going on, on the block until it was my time to step up.

It was 1980 when I started selling weed in school. I already had respect on the ends, so it was easy for me to build my business there, then when I was moving at a certain level I moved on to the front line. I had learnt the basics from my elders, so I was good shotting (selling) weed. But my problem in the beginning was, sometimes I would come up short, true I would mismanage my money. This happened a few times before my Big Man (Boss) got pissed off with me. I was really taking advantage of the fact that his younger brother was my best friend Rico. *Rico and his brothers were Island Boys like me*. We had connected in school because one day he had got suspended for acting up. This was like mid-day. When I was leaving school hours later, my man was still there at school leaning up on the fence just crying. When I looked in his eye, I saw myself right there. His Dad had him shook the same way my Dad had me and right there he became my boy. But even though we were tight and we had been tight for a little while now, the reality was, these man I was running with and working for were members of the Notorious Shower Posse, a Jamaican crew that had been headlining the news around the time for all the wrong reasons. They killed people!

The fact that he was the younger brother to the Big Man really didn't matter. Anyone could get it, even Rico's uncle who was only 5 years older than us. He would teef his step Dad's weed. His step Dad decided to catch him in the act and when Rico's uncle came again, man was in the yard waiting for him. They tied him up and tortured him before shooting him in his face. I went to that Wake and that was the first time I saw the dead body of someone I knew. It made me know this game is serious, but it was the only way I saw to make money. Luckily, boss man just decided to knock my door to get his money back. My Dad answered and they had words, then he went away. When I saw him next, I made him know that I wasn't taking the piss and I would come good, so he allowed me to keep going.

After that I started respecting the ting and doing proper business. *I was born to be a boss*. It didn't take long before I got to the stage where I was moving ounces of weed a day, ready for the reload. I had fought my way to the top in my local area, so my Island Boys and the Project Yutes respected me and my hustle. That was good because users and dealers were getting robbed and set up everywhere. The guys my age couldn't manage me and after a while, even the older yutes from other schools and projects who came to rob guys at my School would just call me a bad "Mother Fucker". They had seen me do my thing and I was proud of the fact that they knew I was a problem. Some of them were blatantly bigger than me, but they would just leave me alone. Even though they would have been able to take my tings, they knew I would have given them all a fight. *Lose or lose.*

1981

That was my life day in day out, selling weed, ramping and getting punch up by the elders. I was at my Step Mum's house all now and things were alright there, but I decided it would make sense if I went and lived with my Dad. It was only about 20 minutes' walk down the road, so I could still see "Mum" when I wanted to. I just wanted a change of scenery really and that was where I was doing most of my business.

The only problem was the witch, but I didn't care anymore. I asked my Dad and he said, 'Alright cool.' So, he enrolled me into the school up the road from him and that was me. This time now, I've already got my crew, the Island Boys. The Project Yutes were hating on us hard now because as we had got older, it was plain to see the difference in how we lived. Us with our town houses compared to the Project Yutes with their food stamps. Us Islands Boys had to stick together because of that. *I remember my first experience of racism wasn't the racist whites, it was the project yutes calling me and my crew coconuts, telling us we need to go home.* This was black on black crime that should have never happened. They should have wanted to learn from us and our culture because we were an extension of them, but they were all so brainwashed, they thought that their culture was right and we were lost. It was something like when white people tried to tan, but at the same time called us niggers because of our melanated skin. The Project Yutes would talk a lot of shit about us but when summer came, *they wished they had the money to holiday in the Caribbean.*

The other cause for contention was the American girls, true they loved us.

This was one school where I didn't have to fight to make friends. The fights I was getting into here in the beginning was because of prejudice. The Project Yutes had been taught that anything before what they had in the project was late and the best thing that happened to them was slavery. Us Island Boys were in the same boat, but saw it from a slightly different perspective.

I always saw the benefits in unity amongst our people, even though I was an Island Boy in their eyes. I always looked for our common ground because we could build on and unify around that and unity was the most important thing, over everything including religion.

I found it in dancing and when the Project Yutes found out that I could body pop, true that was an "American thing", the Project Yutes took to me. They even went as far as letting me into their house, to eat dinner with them and their families. I was the only Island Boy that was allowed in and could walk through to use the train station on the other side of the projects; none of my other friends could do that. If anyone else tried and got caught, they could have got left for dead in them Brookline projects, depending on who caught them slipping.

So all now, it's school, true it's cold we ain't in the park playing Basket Ball so much, but we always on the front line selling drugs. The guys looking food (weed) would meet me where ever I was. This particular winter we had serious snowfall, so we would play snowball fights. One day I was coming out of school playing snowball fights and you didn't wanna get hit with one because man would put stones in them. This is why I was really trying to get away from my boy, not looking as I run into the road. In that moment a car hit me middle stride and all I remember was seeing this woman looking at me as I flew into the air. I knew this was going to be bad, as I started falling. Bang! I landed square on my chin. Licked out my two front teeth in front of all my school friends, it was a bad look. I got up quickly, picked up my teeth, then headed back into the school. I showed them what I had done and they called an ambulance to take me to Brookline Hospital. The school phoned my dad as well and the first thing he said when he got to the hospital was, 'you see what you do to me Mark?' I had to think about that one, cos I was the one who now needed root canal. *He must've meant, I had worried him like maybe I done it on purpose.*

Other than that, life was pretty basic until another one of Rico's older brothers got out of Ryker's Island Prison. He was a Shower Posse General. When he touched road, the game changed a little. Only 19 he was, but he had big man all 30 years and older shook of him. A real killer and I respected that! They were literally saluting him when he came through. Big established man would hide their tings when they heard he was coming and it was shocking to me. He was quite tall, but he was a skinny guy, so I really couldn't believe the weight he had on road and at such a young age.

The first time I met him, he was taxing my bredrin's so he could go to the herb gates as we called it, to get some weed. These guys he was taxing were guys that I looked up to and had ratings for. I had heard about him when he was in jail, but he didn't look like how the road had talked about him. So when he turned to me and asked me what I've got, I just kissed my teet on him and turned my back. He took that as a diss, so he came over and leaned me over a hedge, while he gave me two box (punches).

I told him, 'Get the fuck off me,' as he shrugged me away. Instantly I posed up to fight him, so he looked at me in shock and said, 'Wait, wait you whan fight?'

I said, 'Yeah,' and happily rushed him because I knew after this, my ratings were going through the roof. I did a little side step and he rass me, he hit me so hard I flew across the street. I came back again with a next step, trying another angle and he rass me again, I flew back across the street, then I gave it another go, same ting again. Rass back across the street, then you could say I had enough, *Big Man had taught me a lesson*. I had to worry about my two front teeth getting lick out again. They had put them back in, but told me that my teeth would fall out again at some point so I had to be careful. After the licks I got I went home and looked at my face. I had bumps and bruises all over it and it hurt, but my pride more than anything, true he hadn't licked my teeth back out. My best friend Rico heard what happened and chatted to him when he got home. Big Man said, 'out of all them little pussy holes, he was the only one that did stand up and fight me, I rate that still.' The fact that he said that gave me a lot of ratings in the hood and I became part of their family after that, so elders on the block had to think about fucking with me even more now because he became my extra back up. *He was as real as they came in the hood, an OG!*

Rebelling

Chapter 3

Home life with Dad around the time wasn't easy because of the witch. He would always take her side and they say blood is thicker than water? I don't think so. She still just couldn't wait to tell my Dad anything bad I had done, to get me in trouble. I felt like she was trying to get rid of me, so she could have my Dad all to herself. By now we had been through a lot with my Step Mum and this witch. I could see the change in him, being with this woman.

Now I was really doing things I shouldn't have been doing, the relationship between me and my Dad began to get worse. His own problems had him short tempered and the things I was doing definitely were not helping, so when the witch told him fuckery, he would go in on me hard, with serious licks (beatings). On top of giving me a curfew telling me, 'come in at 10pm.' I'm a big boy now selling weed, making my own money so I would rebel and break that and come in at 11 or 12. When he saw that I was breaking the curfew, it was more licks and now I had to come in at 9. That was a joke ting, so I would take the licks and come in at whatever time I liked, until in the end he just told me I couldn't go out.

This was actually preparing me for bird (jail) as a yute. I ain't gonna lie, sometimes I would do things that deserved punishment, but at first, I was doing stuff as a mischievous yute, then as time went on to get money and rebel.

I stepped up my criminal activity around the time when me and a few bredrins were talking shit and just fucking around. Someone dared us to burgle our school. It started off as a joke, but the fun of me and Delroy talking about it, soon turned into us deciding to do it. Rob our school for their video recorders, all the computers, speakers and anything else that would sell.

When we decided to do it, it was a winter's night, cold and shit so there weren't many people on road. Before we left school for the day, I left the window we were going to be climbing through, slightly open and went about my business. When I was supposed to be in my yard on curfew, I'm out climbing through the classroom window. The security was weak, so we were in and out quickly. We had one of our elders outside with a van, that we filled before we rolled out, happy with how easy it was and how clean we thought we had got away. We sold the tings we stole that same night and went to school the next day like we didn't know anything, acting dumb. We were nice for about a week, then I'm not sure how we got caught but someone called my name, and it didn't take long before the boy dem turned up at my door and told my Dad what I had done, while they were arresting me. They took me in and because I was under age, they hand cuffed me to an iron rail, instead of locking me up in the cells. But the worse part was, my Dad had to come to the court house to get me. When he got me out he told me, 'Make your own way home.' I knew what I was going to get when I got home and I didn't want that, so I decided that I'm running away.

I ended up at Rico's yard, with him and Big Man's Mum and Dad hiding me for the night. The next day I went school as normal but in the evening, Rico's Mum told me, 'You need to go home.' But I wasn't ready for what it seemed like my Dad was looking forward to giving me, so I didn't go home. I ended up in the park where we played ball, sleeping at the bottom of a slide, until I heard, 'Mark, Mark, wake up!' It was my Dad.

That night he clocked how scared I was, so he actually allowed me and didn't give me the beating I was due to get.

After that I hoped things would get better with me and him,

but they didn't. All I wanted was my super hero to spend more time with me. Be that Dad to me I loved because boys need their Dads more than anything. But it came like ground hog day! At least once a week I would get caught with the weed I was selling and my punishment was always licks (beatings).

My Dad would beat me like weed was the worst thing in the world and true he didn't smoke, I accepted it. I carried on doing it though because I was becoming very rebellious and this was just another something I done at the time to rebel.

Jamaica

It was summer time again and I was big 17. My Dad decided it had been a while since we had been Jamaica, so he booked us all a family trip. It was me him and the witch he had married without telling me all those years ago. *That still hurt my feelings!* They got a hotel room from they landed and left me with my Uncle to do my ting, but now I was grown I didn't care.
I linked my same bredrin Purnel from back in the day and now we both smoked weed, so we went for it first thing. He took me down to his spot in the middle of the hood. I got my ting and I got a ting for him, proper high grade. I was a smoker and Jamaica was the home of the high grade, so this holiday was all about getting high. I had to acclimatise to that shit though. Anytime I hit it in that first week I needed to sleep for a few hours, but after that I was nice.

I saw that holiday as my Dad's way of telling me sorry for some of what he had done to me, but even more than that, it was a holiday for him and his wife. I didn't even stay in the hotel with them once. I would just link them when I was reloading on my money, or we were linking on a one-a-way to go to a family event. That holiday Purnel was my roll dawg. He took me raving and we watched one or two gal, but I didn't fuck none of them.

I had a good time that holiday, but the holiday went quick and I knew by now that when I got back to the ends, my Dad was going to go back to his old ways to, so it was what it was.

Weed

Back home we hadn't been back from Jamaica for that long and things were alright. I had finished High School with some half decent grades. *Imagine after everything, if I had a little support what I could have achieved.* I had been doing so well I actually had dreams of becoming a Pilot. I hadn't been able to do that though because my maths grade hadn't been good enough, but they were better than average, so I had been accepted into The New York College of Printing, which was still quite prestigious back then. I had agreed to go even though I didn't want to because I knew it would make my Dad happy. The College was in Manhattan, so I would wake up early morning to travel down there each day. The first day I got there, I saw one of my old school friends from down by the 40's. He was in my class, I couldn't believe it because it had been so long since I had seen him. Now he was part of the 5 Percenters, which were an off shoot from the Nation of Islam. Clever as well as serious, so no one fucked with them and they were a crew that stayed to themselves. Basically, me and him weren't even supposed to be friends, but because we knew each other from long time and we were coming way off the ends to Manhattan to study in the same class, we were cool. We needed to hang with each other too because us as Brooklyn boys weren't cool with the Harlem and Bronx boys, for no other reason than we were from different areas, so they didn't like us on their block.

From the first day, they were running Brooklyn man off the ends after class, with knives and chains. The only reason they left us was because my bredrin was rolling fully loaded and he didn't mind who knew it. After I saw that on my first day, I didn't see myself staying there for long, so the next day I brought my weed in and started serving up (selling drugs). I was the drug dealer and my bredrin was my gunman back up.

That worked well for a little while, but seeing how serious these Harlem and Bronx boys were trying to fuck up us Brooklyn boys I knew I couldn't stay there too long. If I wasn't with my man for example, they would have been trying to run me off the ends like they were running everyone else and that couldn't work.

So after a few weeks I decided to just cool and enrol on the ends in my local Brooklyn College where everything was normal, and I could do my ting in peace. Sell my weed, chill on the block, play my ball and be with the man dem. My Dad wasn't happy that I left that college, but he didn't know what I was going through over there, so he wasn't really in a position to judge me even though he always had something to say, with the help from that witch.

My love for weed was the main cause for contention those days. Weed was the worst thing in the world to my Dad, he would say things like, 'You leave big college to become neighbourhood drug dealer? Not in my house.' If he found weed on me, he would flush it down the toilet, or just take it as well as give me a beating. This was going on for months, playing cat and mouse with my Dad over my weed.

In our house we had a basement, it was like a studio downstairs with a party room in one section, music equipment in a next section and a section that was off limits to me. I always wondered why I wasn't allowed in that section. My Dad would have all his people down in there and it always sounded like a party, when I heard them selecting big old school tracks. I was my Dad's Prince in his own words, when he wasn't beating me, so I wondered what he was hiding from me in that part of the basement where everyone always seemed to have so much fun.

One day, I decided I was going to see for myself what they were doing down there, that was such a secret. There was windows that were used as air vents all around the basement on the ground level, so I went outside, laid on the floor and looked in. When I say I couldn't believe it, my Dad was down there with a big blunt in his hand smoking and talking about weed deals. After all the licks I had got for smoking weed, all this time my Dad had been smoking weed too. I was so angry and hurt; my Dad was such a hypocrite. I wanted to do him something so bad, but what could I do? I had to leave it, but anytime anyone tried it in college or on road, they were getting it. I would wild out when I was fighting. I wasn't losing none of my fights now because that was my opportunity to do something. These were the licks I really wanted to give my Dad.

On road now true The Big Man was back, everyone was working for him. Us youngers were just selling weed, but we all wanted to step up to get closer to him. *He was just a Bad Man, straight*. He was a robber, drug dealer boss, that never worked a day in his life but always looked fresh to death. If you weren't selling drugs for him on the ends, you would hide your tings, run or just get robbed when he came around. Guys might have acted like he wasn't that bad when he wasn't there, but none of them said that to his face cos they knew he would humiliate them and that was anybody.

I Think I know It All At 17 1983

I had lost a lot of respect for my Dad with that last lie I had caught him in. I couldn't do him anything, but I was getting to that age where I wasn't as scared as I used to be. He had told me to come in early because I was on curfew again but, fuck that. I'm out with the man dem chilling as we walking to Pathmark, a local grocery store to get some Dunkin Donuts. It was about 11.30pm and I knew I was in trouble, but that was nothing new. I didn't care until we heard a car that sounded like my Dad's car rolling up behind us. My neighbour Leroy said, 'Oh shit,' and that's when I knew it was my Dad's car screeching to a halt. Of all the Dad's cars it could have been, why mine? I went straight to the car because I didn't want any of my boys to see what was going to happen next. I knew it was a beating. When I got to the car, my Dad pointed to a fan belt that was on the passenger seat.

He said, 'You see that, that's for you, get in.' I looked at it and knew that was gonna hurt, it was black rubber with bare ridges and flexible. It was going to leave a bag of marks in my back. I was scared because I didn't want that, I didn't know what to do because I knew if I tried to run my Dad was going to beat me in front of all my boys, so I got in and as we drove off, he was cussing me all the way to the yard. As he's cussing, I'm trying to hide the belt under the seat. I did manage to hide it lickle piece and that gave me time to try get into the yard, but he did find it quick and get out just in time to block me off by the gate.

Now he's telling me, 'Pass, pass now!' I knew if I try pass him the beating was gonna start from there, so I tried to talk him down.

I said, 'Dad, why you want to always beat me like I'm a stranger. I love you Dad.' He wasn't having none of it.

He said, 'Mark, if you don't come here now, you see that empty milk bottle. I'm gonna buss your head with it. Just come for your licks.'

I said, 'Dad, you talking like you hate me. How you gonna buss my head with the milk bottle? He still wasn't having any of it, so in the end I tried to pass him.

With each step I picked up my pace, until by the time I was close to him I was almost running. The first lick he gave me did catch me on my back as I passed, and wow it did hurt. *He was using imagination to give me licks now.* I run up the stairs to the front door and tried to open it, but it was locked. I'm two storeys up; its either I jump, or I face him again trying to get back down. I had to face him, and this is where he did catch me with bare licks. I could feel blood streaming from my back with every new lick. Neighbours were moving curtains to see what was going on because they could hear me screaming. It's a summer night, road still active. Two gal that went to my college were on their porch watching. I'm just getting licks all now. I can't get in the house and I can't pass him and these girls are laughing like they can't wait to get to college tomorrow to tell everyone. I hate you now Dad, you making me look like a fool in front of my peers. The beating lasted about 5 minutes, it wasn't no quick ting. These beatings I would get were workouts for both of us and as time had gone on, my threshold for licks had improved til I didn't cry anymore, and he wanted to see me cry, so he would beat me more and more each time. This time though I refused to cry because I knew that's what he wanted. When he felt like he had beat me enough, he let me go into the house where I went straight to my bedroom to look at my wounds and sort myself out. Vex as I'm looking at all the wets (cuts) he gave me with that fan belt or improvised weapon. *He took the piss and in front of people.* Our relationship changed forever that night. From then I said fuck it, I took to the streets even more because I really saw it like; people on the streets were more my family than him. If he can treat me like this, how do I need to look at my enemies? I didn't fear no one on road, but he wants me to fear him. "Fuck that", Town House yutes are my family now, that's all.

The street elders took me in and became like my Uncles after that and they would let us chill with them from time to time. Them man were like four or five years older than us, so we felt real when they let us chill with them. We would play ball together, smoke weed and reason. They would tell us all about the madness they got up to and that was when I first saw cocaine. Some of the elders were taking it. *That was what they were doing to show the levels.* The Big Man done it as well and for me as a yute man for him, I was just impressed at how he had big bad boy elders even older than him, soft. Whatever he said, is what it was. He lived the life all the way. I had mad respect and love for him like a big brother for how he moved, so when he told us he was going to court, we were all pissed. *They ended up sending him back to jail for another 2 years or so.*

It was business as usual though, just part of us growing getting desensitised to jail. *One of our elder going back.* When he went away that time, one of his bredrins, Bully took over the street ting. I knew Bully's younger brother Raymond. He didn't go my school, but we would link up, smoke weed and play basketball together after school. He was a next man that would drop food (drugs) on me too, to help me eat. But as time went on, Bully became the guy I would get my food from when Big Man went away as he was the new boss. *We all wanted to be with and around the boss.*

Tings was alright with Bully in the beginning. He would get the food in from his older brother who brought it up from Florida; boxes of Cocaine and Weed. He was getting it directly from the Columbians, Pablo's people when Pablo was on top of the world. Bully was big because he didn't just have us man working for him, he was security for a big club in New York at the time so he would sell cocaine there too.

One day, my bredrin Wise who was working the weed ting with me came short on Bully's money. We were all in the park chilling when Wise saw him. He was so shook he didn't even wait for Bully to ask him where his money was, he was just gone. Bully did catch him a few days later and rough him up, but by that time Wise had his money so it wasn't so bad. A week later it was my time to pay up. I was correct with the money but Bully miscounted, so he told me I was short. I knew I was right so I held my ground. As he hooked me in my face, two hook. I held that, then he took out his borer. I looked at him thinking, nah he's not gonna do that, but he did. He wet me in my face from the top of my eye down deep into my cheek. From there he said a few more words then he let me go, so I went to go patch up my wound. As I was walking I heard that familiar car engine, it was my Dad, so straight away it was on top. I got in the car and he drove me to Brookdale Hospital, where they gave me 14 stitches in my face. After that the talk was, my Dad had enough and he was sending me to London. I couldn't say anything, so now I only have a few days left in Brooklyn. It was Friday and I was leaving on Monday, so I spent my last days smoking weed with the man dem and reasoning.

Before I knew it, it was Monday and I was being sent to Kennedy Airport to leave and go back to London.

Chapter 4

I touched down in London, this new land I didn't know. I got picked up from the airport and taken to my Grandad's yard der in Hackney. As I got out the car, my Grandad was there with a big smile waiting for me. *It was nice to see a friendly face for real. I never went school here, so I don't know anyone.* He told me how he remembered me as a yute, but now I was grown he was treating me more like a bredrin.

He told me about his life before he went to the army and all the gal he used to fuck with. He was even alright with me smoking weed.

All he said was, 'if Ms Marsha's around then don't smoke, but if she isn't then bring me in.'Cool! Day to day he was like the family babysitter and he would watch my younger Brother and Sister while my Mum went to work because she was still a Nurse and their Dad, my stepdad was a Bus Driver.

I didn't get the best vibe from my stepdad though. He didn't even answer me when I spoke, he would just grunt and when he was at home, all I saw him do was sit down by the window, watching cricket and his Volvo. He loved that car so much, I thought he wasn't serious, me coming from NY where we had some real serious cars.

Furthermore, it didn't take long before I realised he just didn't like me. It might have been because I was my Mum's first, or I was just the reminder of her life before him that he didn't want to remember. *From that I just wanted to go home because it was better the devil you know.*

I had been in London now for about two weeks and there were some girls that lived on my Mum's road I would check when I was around. I had got this ghetto blaster that needed a new plug and thought I'd asked them if I could borrow a screwdriver to sort out. They had one so it wasn't a problem, I got the screwdriver, borrowed it then brought it back in the evening and that's when my friend told me, 'You've got a secret admirer you know.' There was a girl there at the time I didn't noticed noticing me.

I was like 'Is it, bring me in then.' So they made the link and me and her started talking. We had tings in common from the start cause her Dad was in New York and she was just about to leave to go, but she was only going for a few weeks, so we talked and said that we would carry on talking when she got back.

When she got back I realised I liked her, so I told her I wanted her to be my girlfriend. She said she would think about it, then the next day, she came back to me and said, 'Yes, I want to be your girl.' Then she introduced me to her family. She had one older brother, one younger brother and a younger sister.

London became more interesting then, not that I was watching London, I was more watching my girl. As time went on and I got comfortable on the ends, the same friend that linked me up with my girl, her older cousin linked me up with a weed man called Moveaff. I hadn't smoked weed for about 4 months because I didn't know where to get it, but now me link Moveaff, me nice.

After a while, I started going to his yard to chill without her. Moveaff was cool and he would help where he could, so when his bredrin offered him a job, he said 'Yes,' and he did bring me in too. It was sales and off the books, so that was an extra touch.

Tings were good at that job for a few weeks as well, until I decided to bring the Boss to my yard to meet my Mum, so she could see I was trying to do good and I was really working. First of all, I met her husband at the front door as he was washing his car. I introduced him to my boss and then we went towards the house where my Mum stopped us at the door. She didn't even let him in so we were there talking for a while, with my boss explaining what I do and after that he kept it moving. I went in and me and my Mum were talking for a while in the kitchen, then my stepdad came in. He called my Mum into the front room and left me in the kitchen, then my Mum came back a few minutes later saying,

'Mark, I hope it's not true you know?'

I said, 'What Mum?'

She said, 'Roy said he saw your boss down by Baker's Arms selling ash.' He was lying; my Boss was an honest Muslim man who didn't even take drugs. I was pissed because this is the same thing my Dad's wife used to do, tell my Dad stuff to get me in trouble. Now my Mum's husband was doing the same thing; trying to push me out. I started cussing off Roy so Roy started acting bad like he's gonna do me something. He went upstairs for something to beat me with and I stayed downstairs waiting. He was upstairs for a while banging around, acting like he was trying to find it, but I knew he wasn't going to do shit.

After a while, he came to the top of the stairs and said, 'Look, I can't find it, but this is my house and if you're going to act like that, you can get out.'

My Mum, instead of backing me said, 'Yes Mark, you need to come out of the house.' I couldn't believe it, that broke my heart. Right there I left the yard and went to live with my Missus in her Mum's house and they became my family. Me and Moveaff stayed at the job until it flopped a few months later, but we had built a good relationship with each other, so we would socialise together and smoke in our local snooker hall, where we would play Kalooki, pool and snooker.

I was still trying to fit in and stay out of trouble, so I took agency work packing in warehouses and other shit jobs for a while. *I was crime free other than the weed*. But linking different man at that snooker hall started giving me options on the ends, for my weed if I didn't see Moveaff, and other things.

I'd been in London six months now, but I was still talking to my boys back home. They would tell me new stuff that was going on, I was missing so I holla'd my Dad and asked him if I could come back. He must have missed me a little bit too because he thought about it for a bit, then sorted out my ticket. *I was on my way back to Brooklyn!*

When I landed I thought I would have got back into the stride of Brooklyn life. I bucked (linked) up my best friend; but now he had a new best friend. It felt like I'd died, and my spirit could see what was going on. *It didn't feel like home again.* He was going Canarsie High School now and I would link him on the American Football pitch on his break. I was introduced as, his bredrin who just come back from England, to all the girls. The first thing they would ask me is, 'What happened to your face?' *Bringing back bad memories.* It was a little embarrassing, but it was always only for a moment. I kept it moving with me bredrin making sure the questions stopped. From there he would go back to class and I would head either to the park, or the front line.

My Dad had organised a motor mechanic ting for me, trying to help, but by that time I didn't want anything he was offering. The streets had me, I actually wanted the road life now! Apart from the fact that, where I was supposed to go to this motor mechanic was in Manhattan. That for me as a "Brooklyn man" on the front line making money every day was long. It seemed like too much work. I'm moving up now to robberies too and "Bully" who had wet me in my face, realised he fucked up and apologised for it. Even though he had marked my face for life, at least he acknowledged it, so that made things on road a little better.

Everything was alright now I was back in Brooklyn, until I did rob one yute and he turned up at my Dad's yard. I didn't know how this guy knew where I live, but now he was flaming up my ting. My Dad had to break him off some P's (money) because he was talking about going to the police, it was very messy. Things had changed in Brooklyn! So I started to see London as an attractive alternative. In the 6 months I'd been there, I had put on over a stone in weight, I had my girl there and I had just learned she had terminated our baby because she didn't know what I was doing, if I was even coming back. My Dad had sent her the money to get the termination, but it was playing on my mind, as well as the fact that I've got my younger brothers and sister there that I want to get to know. I didn't want to keep making mess for my Dad either, so I asked him if I could go back to London and he felt like that was a good idea, so within the next week I was on my way back.

As soon as I got back, the first door I knocked on was my Missus. She didn't know I was back, so when her Mum opened the door and saw me standing there then called her, all I saw was teeth. She was so happy to see me, she ran and just jumped into my arms.

I had used my Grandad's house phone to call Brooklyn when I had come to London the first time, and the bill had come in crazy, so my Grandad's wife, Ms Marshall had told him that I couldn't stay there again. *Shit was going to be different this time*. They told me, 'You should go and stay in an under 21's hostel and after a while you will get your place.' But I didn't feel ready to stay in no hostel, so I went and stayed at my girlfriend's house. But as a young man, my family was right and I needed my own spot, so I decided to go and do the hostel ting after staying with my girls family for a while.

There was a guy at this hostel, that hit the road every day from early robbing people. He would come home with a bag of tings every day so after seeing that for a few days. I told him, 'Bring me in!' I wanted in on some of that road money, so he took me Highbury and Islington the next day and the first man we saw, we robbed.

I was on him like, 'Yo Man, what's good?' In my American accent as I approached him, headlock, my guys peeled out his pockets and we left. It was the first crime I did in England and it was easy. It was a lickle eat still, we made a quick £250 which was alright back then and after that we came back to the ends, got some weed and chilled.

After the success of that first move, we ran that day in day out and I saw the fear in people's eye when I spoke. I knew it was wrong and if I had a better option I would have taken it, but we weren't just given good options on the ends, so I was getting in where I fitted in. I didn't do it every day and those days when I wasn't robbing guys, I chilled with the Missus.

I was beginning to enjoy my social life in London and I started to venture out. Now I knew a few man on the ends, we would link up at our local Youth Centre. Every area had at least one and it was here where I would see man playing basketball. As an American that was my ting, so I played and that's when people saw what I was really about. I was a baller and man would have to tag team me. At times there were 3 man trying to take me on, even trying to trip me up, I was that good.

As well as that, some of the man in the crew were on this boxing ting and that was my other comfort zone. I didn't have the stamina like them man because of all the smoking, but they could see I had the angles. Yeah, the ends started to be alright and I started to see who was who. The majority of man in the circle were teef (thieves), so fast money became the only money and that's where the next phase in my life began.

The guy that I had started robbing with finally got a place from the council. *In my mind we had become a team.* Now he had his place, I felt like we had a place and I didn't like all the rules and regulations living in the hostel; it come like lockdown. I always thought, why the fuck should I come in when they tell me. Well, needless to say, it didn't take long before I was on my last warning, then I was getting kicked out. I needed Kevin now, the guy I had done the robberies with. He had a yard I could use, so I asked him but he said "NO!" I was hurt by the way he elbowed me out and locked me off. *Reject he whan reject me yeah, Ok, I'm going to make him suffer when I see him, it's very simple!* That's the way I thought, even though he didn't really owe me anything.

In the meantime, I had to go YMCA and stay there to try get my flat. My Missus would come and check me there every day and all we did was fuck. So before I knew it surprise surprise, the Missus was pregnant again. This put more pressure on me, but instead of staying in the YMCA and waiting for my yard, my Missus's Mum invited me back to her yard and I moved back in with her.

All now I'm doing petty crime in Walthamstow market because I was working with a weak team. I couldn't link the guys I needed to link like the Armed Robber man and the big drug dealers, whilst I was on road with these guys because they didn't

have any ratings. The temp work ting wasn't working for me. It wasn't consistent so I had a lot of time on my hands and I didn't have to act like I was trying to be good now cos I wasn't seeing my Mum.
I was seeing man dem cut serious paper in front of me. *I wanted some of that money.*

A few of the older man got out of jail around the time. I was rolling with a man called Sherman. He was a car thief and burglar but he would put it on you too if he had to, but he wasn't really a fighting man. He was more a thief and a Sound Man. But his brother, Nevil. He was more like the man dem from back home that did big birds and came out. When he touched road, not even a week later, he had a new whip (car). That got my attention! *Nevil and his team were out and about.* He would touch Hackney, Tottenham and South London and sometimes they would totally leave the ends on moves. This is what I was on, broadening my horizons. Nevil and his crew were Armed Robber (AR) specialists, they would mainly rob security vans, but banks could get it too. That's what they had gone in for and they must have had money put down, or done a new job straight away because they were back with a bang quickly and now, I was riding shot gun. I was official on the ends because everyone respects them guys.

This is around the time Marcia gave birth to my first born, Owen. I couldn't believe I was a Dad now, it was emotional. *I regret not going to watch my baby being born.* I waited in the car. I was just going with this as a road man. Marcia had already got rid of one of our children, so we couldn't do that again, but it didn't change the fact that I didn't feel ready for a yute. It wasn't long after Marcia gave birth that she got a flat in Chingford and over night we were virtually living together as Husband and Wife. The next problem was, I wasn't ready for the life of Husband and Wife either and what my Dad said all those years ago was ringing in my head.

In one of the arguments he had with my step Mum, he told me mid argument, 'Mark, don't ever get married you know.' Marcia was evolving but I wasn't and I began to get a little jealous of our baby. It was more the fact that before little man, it was all about me, but now my Missus wasn't all about me anymore. Little man was in the middle. Marcia wanted me around all the time on top of that, but our crying baby was hurting my head, so I chose to be on the road. *Children both parents aren't ready for always make a relationship harder, especially if you don't have a consistent way to provide, so the pressure was on.* Before I was teefing for me and Marcia, but now little man was here needing shit, my crimes needed to feed all of us.

Jail

I had been in London two years now and I hadn't linked my cousin Gary since I'd last seen him in Brooklyn. He was still up in Northampton so it wasn't that close, but one weekend I decided I was going to go link him. The Missus hadn't been giving me too much trouble, but I was feeling like I needed to do something and I was a teef, so it was a teefing ting. Anywhere I went I would teef, so when I got to Northampton and my cousin linked me, he showed me wha gwan and who's who on the ends as we drove around in my cousin's little banger.

We drove past this prestigious car show room and as I looked at all these nice cars, I told my cousin to stop. Walking around the show room, I noticed a nice Mercedes with it's keys in the door. *I couldn't believe it*. I opened it and got in, turned the ignition and it turned on. I pushed it in first gear and it moved off. All they had was a little chain on a latch that I could open to release and I did. Then I shouted to my cousin, 'I'll LINK YOU BACK!' and I was off, heading to the motorway, trying to drive this whip back to the ends to sell. I was feeling real all now driving this whip down the motorway, speeding 120 mph. I was driving so fast that as I came up to my turn off to London, I had to slam on the breaks, but still missed the turning. True it was only a little bit and I wasn't familiar with the area, I decided to reverse on the motorway instead of continuing straight like I should have. As I did the illegal manoeuvre on big M1, the police were at the top of the road watching the whole thing. The pussy holes stopped me straight, questioned me. I tried to speech it, but they weren't having any of it. I even had my thieving tool kit in the car, *I had no chance*. I was going straight to jail. They took me back to Northampton Police Station and the next day I went Court, where I was remanded and taken back to the cells, until the meat wagon come to take me Glen Parva jail, in Leicester. *I was pissed, as you can imagine.*

This was my first time really going to jail. It was an under 21's facility with straight 23 hour bang up. No TV or toilet in your cell. So any TV you wanted to watch you had to go to the communal to watch. *This cell was good for push ups, sit ups and bed.*

I'd heard a lot of stories of jail, so in my mind I expected it pretty much exactly how it was and I'd heard a lot worse stories, so this was alright as far as jails went. Three days in and all was alright, until one guy decided to try take the piss.

I had my fag on my ear and he took it and went about his business. It was a test that I wasn't having so I followed him to his cell where I confronted him.

I said, 'YO, WHAT YOU DOING TRYING TO TAKE MY SHIT. GIVE ME BACK MY SHIT NOW.' He didn't do anything and I got my shit back so I left it at that, but he had to respect me. He was running the wing, so he didn't know any better than to take people's shit, but he wasn't taking mine. That was the only situation I had before my Grandad bailed me out. He paid £750 to Northampton Magistrate's Court and I was thankful to him for real, *he was my bredrin.*

When I got back to the ends and told man dem what happened, they respected that. I was moving up the ranks because I had left the ends on my own, way up in the Midlands and almost got away with the big ting, I was taking risks!

1986

They gave me probation for that, but I didn't care. It was back to normal straight away. My little bro was coming up around the time with his little crew and they were always talking about they need P's. One day I decided to show them how to get it by any means and sent them on their way, to make a mess of the streets they were in, creating more ripple effects, I didn't know about at the time. I taught them to rob man, steal cars and don't have it.

A few weeks later I decided to steal a next car to use when I was driving to rave. *It was a Ford Capri 3 litre ting.* I did bend back the car door enough to open it, then when I was in I bent it back. I buss off the panel underneath the steering wheel and just like in the movies connected the two wires. After a few seconds it fired up and we were ready to go. Now I've got this whip, I linked me bredrin Freddie and we went to this party in Leytonstone. We were there for a while but it was dead inside, so we decided to leave there and see what was on road to teef. As we were driving on the ends the boy dem see us. *It was racial profiling even though the car was stolen.*

I had a choice all now, it's either I stop and stay there for them to question us and go to jail, or we keep it moving and try to get away. I decided to keep it moving, so they followed and it quickly turned into a police chase. They chased me up and down the ends until I got to a path way near Essex Road, Leyton, where I tried to block the path with the car, so the police would have to give chase on foot. *I knew I was getting away if they had to chase me on foot.* Freddie got out and run one way and I got out and ran in a different direction, but because I was the driver they were on me. The pussy holes were able to drive past the car too, so they continued driving behind me, while I'm on foot. Pissed! *So I decided to act like I'm tired.* When they got out and came for me, I took off running. They must have thought, *fuck this guy* as they got back into the car, because with no hesitation they just ran me over. Knocked me way up into the air and when I landed they took my broke up ass to jail.

This time I got sent to Chelmsford Prison. Where I was the oldest in this youth offenders facility. But they only gave me 4 months. *I saw that as alright for real*. I had stolen a car and got into a police chase. If that was the kind of punishments I could expect, why not be a criminal coz I knew I wasn't going to get caught all the time.

Chapter 5

The first day I got there, everyone was asking me if I was fit.

I asked 'Why?'

They said, 'The screws will make us all suffer, if you can't keep up.' *Fuck that*! But when it was time for our circuit, I saw what they were talking about. *Even though in my mind these screws weren't gonna have me up.* They put us in pairs and told us that we all had to keep up, or we were all going to do it again. *This prison come like army.* When this screw told me he wanted me to sprint to a post, which was quite far away, the guy I was paired with sprinted, but I just ran as normal. When the screw saw I wasn't trying, he put it on me and made me know that I better do what he says or everyone's going to suffer. It was a peer pressure ting that worked. *Punishments in this jail were excessive ironing and marching like we were in army training*, so I got it after that and ran like I was supposed to, *impressively as well I might add.*

This jail was an open prison and I could have just left, but I had my family I was thinking about. If I had run, I wouldn't have been able to spend it with them and I would have been looking over my shoulder until they caught me. *The consequences were very high.*

It was a soft prison, but I was in the hardest part of it and it was only hard because of all the military type business we had to do.

The other side of the prison didn't have a certain time to get up and they didn't have to clean like we did, having everything in our cell spotless. That part of it was so bad, some man just wanted to go to normal jail.

I was there when the Broadwater Farm riots kicked off and Winston Silcott got his life sentence for killing PC Blakelock. I remember it coming through on the radio; that was big news. I did my time in there relatively peacefully because the screws had everything under control so I didn't want to make any waves.

The day I was released, I cried at the thought of seeing my son again. It felt like I hadn't seen him for so long and I had missed him. I jumped in with one of my jail mates who was being released the same day, from Romford, true his Dad came for him and made my way back to the ends with them.

When I got home, we got back to family life and it didn't take long before Marcia was pregnant again. As you can imagine, the pressure of a next yute made me desperate. I needed to do something real quick. The only option I felt like I had available to me was, hit the road harder. The 9 to 5 ting was long, I didn't have any patience for the bullshit. *It was all about fast money.* I had trouble taking orders from funny guys that weren't smart and liked to lord their position of power over people. The same type that would walk past you on road and avoid eye contact, even moving out the way.

Yeah, fuck the 9 to 5 ting I thought. I just needed a better plan, so I decided to just stay on the estate and rob the drug dealer's customers. Who the fuck were they going to run to. It was easy as well because Chingford Hall Estate had a lot of dark spots, in that underground car park and as I'd done a lot already on road, the other bad boys in the area respected me and everybody else feared me.

With this pressure of a new baby coming, every day from when I left my yard I'd be robbing people. Some of them even knew where I lived but I didn't care, I was moving reckless and causing a mess for my family. I'd even started taking people's cars and making them write me a bill of sale, as well as sign over the log book.

I'd shout them as they drove pass, 'YO, pullover!' You could see on man's face, they were thinking what the fuck have I done? But they didn't want to drive off and make me catch them a next day because it was going to be worse for them. So they would pull up and I'd say, 'Where you get this car from?' They would stutter, wondering why I was asking. Then after a little small talk, where I'd tell them how much I liked the car and that they're gonna need to sign over the log book to me, I'd tell them to get out and walk.

Now the Missus was pregnant, she was extra emotional and taking it out on me, so I was extra emotional and taking it out on road. I was causing a bag of ripple effects, I wasn't even thinking about at the time. I didn't care about the problems I was causing my many victims. *It wasn't as simple as me just taking a man's car.* After I humiliated him, left him on the road side to walk and smiled as I drove off in his whip, on top of telling him, 'If you tell the feds, I'm gonna fuck you up.' *Did I think he was going to go home to his wife and kids and be nice? When people laughed at him and called him a pussy for having that big violation, did I think he was going to take it lying down, or was he going to cause the people around him all kind of problems?* I know what I would have done! But because I had become a terrorist on road, I didn't see the after effects of my actions. All I was thinking about was robbing everything that moved, from the customers for their money or weed, to drug dealers I didn't like and even just random public, to robbing so many cars I had my own chop shop, in my own section of our car park. *I had about 25 cars parked up at one stage just there.*

I was taking the piss so guys started talking about, when they see me they going to do me something. I had the local drug dealers pissed because I was stopping them from eating. Guys wouldn't come to the estate because of me, but all I was saying to them was, 'It's either you give me money, or they gonna give me money, I'm getting it daily regardless.' *I had to eat!*

After about 18 months of this, going to jail started to become a norm for thefts, burglaries, carjacking and the fighting once every few months, on little stupid birds.

The Missus had given birth to our Daughter now. Her name

was Kandi and she looked like a 50/50 split between us. The Missus was giving me extra problems because of the lifestyle I was living now. She knew I could go jail or even worse at any time. So she would moan about me leaving the house, like she wanted me to stay in. But then she would complain when I couldn't pay certain bills. I couldn't win, but she definitely didn't want me putting myself at anymore risk coz she knew when I left the house, anything could happen and it usually did. *I was picking up new beef daily, foe and friend alike.*

One of my old bredrin's who turned pussy hole was in line to get it for a start, when I saw him. About he had come to my house telling my baby Mum that when he sees me on road he gonna do me something. This was the same bredrin that, when I went jail last, I had left my car with him. He had taken and sold it to some guy who crashes cars for sport and I hadn't said anything, when I touched road. I just remembered and knew I was going to dark him sooner or later.

My opportunity came one evening when I was coming home. I saw his car parked up and open, so I took it for a spin and wrote it off. *It felt good.* I shouldn't have turned into the first suspect because I didn't say anything to him when he sold my car, but I did and now he was telling my baby mother shit. I was looking for this pussy hard and it didn't take long before I found him either. My Missus had been giving me a lot of problems as well and I needed to release this on someone, so when I saw him, I put it on him straight. He was coming out of the local pub and his weapon was ready. It was the chain from a chain saw, but I didn't care. I had my mini axe and a screw driver and I said, 'I heard you looking for me, I'm here now so let's do it. You were talking a lot of shit to my baby mother, let me hear that shit now.' He froze on me, that chain went limp. The brains behind that weapon weren't saying nothing. He calmed his mouth down and listened to what I had to say. True he didn't really want anything, we kept it moving.

After that my name did ring on road, so much so, most brea's on the ends were afraid to ride with me. I would kick it off (start beef) anywhere in front of anyone. *That was me building my rep.*

I remember a few days after, seeing that yute in Walthamstow Market. The one who hadn't let me stay in his new yard when the hostel pussy holes were trying to evict me. I did beat his rass that day, to teach him a lesson. This was so normal to me, after I beat him I went about my day like absolutely nothing had happened. I didn't even mention it to anyone who wasn't there. A few hours later I was at Norths, our local arcade spot, looking for my next victim, when out of nowhere I felt a tump (a hard hit). I turned around and see this guy that I had just buss up a few hours early, trying to come back for me. None of the guys in Norths had seen what had happened earlier, so it just looked like new beef. Anyway, when I turned and saw this pussy trying to fuck me up, that made me even more mad like, after what I just gave you, you tried to come back for me yeah. He got an extra beating for that!

Things like this were happening every other day, so it didn't take long before I ended up only rolling with man like me. Man that had everyone on road shook, because we respected each other and no one wanted to roll with them man either. There was a few man around the time that were doing things, but The General I did warm to the most. He was my cocaine link getting money daily. I wasn't into cocaine yet, but I wanted in because I was seeing the money man was making from that.

The first day I rolled with him, we hit Four Aces in Dalston Hackney. We rolled up and this yardie in a black suit waved us down. He had food (Cocaine) so we happily pulled over. I was driving The General's car. The General started talking to him and he had exactly what we wanted, so The General took the ting and tasted it. After he tried some, he gave it to me and asked me what I thought. I put it in my mouth and my whole mouth went numb. *It was good food*. The General gave me the nod and I was off. I put my foot to the floor and this guy jumped on the car as he's screaming at us, 'AH WAH DE RASS, PUSSYHOLE AH TRY FE ROB ME. ME WILL KILL UNO BLOODCLART TODAY IN YA.' I was a little surprised with how quick he moved, as I tried to get away. The guy managed to open the door and get in. I'm thinking rass, then he brought out a big knife and started waving it around with a whole heap of BLOODCLART talk. Me and The General were in the front acting cool, but I'm not gonna lie, my heart was beating! After a while with The General talking to him, he calmed down. Imagine, The General told him that we were just about to park up, but with all the madness, the cocaine had fallen onto the floor and was all in the carpet. This yardie wanted to make the sale so bad, he brought out a next ting. I ballsed that ting quickly and told him I lost that too. The Yardie was so mad! I got out the car acting like I'm looking for it and The General was acting like he was getting mad telling me, 'You better find it Yanks.' The Yardie come to realise we've bumped him again, so he got out the car and this is when we were supposed to speed off. The General got into the driver's seat as the Yardie got out and I went around to the passenger's side. As I'm getting into the whip, the Yardie went across the road to where some bricks were piled up. The General wasn't sure what he was gonna do next, so he was distracted as we went to make our escape. We crashed into a fence then crashed into another fence, it was a disaster of a getaway! In this time the Yardie picked up a brick and hurled it at us. Now we were ducking and driving as it smashed out our back window. We buss one left and then a quick right and got out of there, heading back to the ends. As we drove down Lea Bridge Road The General asked me, 'Was you scared Yanks?'

I said, 'No.' then asked him if he was and he said,

'I was you know,' then laughed a Frank Bruno type laugh that made me think, this guy is crazy. As we went back to one of our safe houses to wash up the cocaine. This was the first time I saw cocaine turn to crack and it was the first time I smoked it. *It left me prang (on edge)*. That's how the crack got me. If I had known the dirty life it was going to take me down, I would have run far from that and The General. I thought about that Yardie and how he was really on us. Now we had done that and The General saw I was on this ting, he turned into a different kind of big man and this is where tings turned a little crazy.

We finished that food and he said in his deep husky voice,

'You know what Yanks?'

In my mind I knew exactly what he wanted to do but I waited for it, HE LOVED IT.

'We got to go back on the road and do another move!' This time we linked up with, let's call him, Little Bigger Man. He was at a yard we stopped at to see wha gwan and this is when I see a next side to The General. Little Bigger Man was a few years older than us and he was a next level killer. He walked everywhere with a 10 inch blade in a newspaper and if he moved to you and you didn't have anything for him, you was going to get poked. He had killed bare guys already, so it wasn't easy to say no when he asked us to take him West. He told us we can get some food there as well so we were actually even on it! But as we drove West, I noticed this isn't the same General now. Little Bigger Man is in control of our surroundings.

We got to Ladbroke Grove and went into one house, I stayed in the front room as Little Bigger Man was talking with The General, in the kitchen. I didn't hear what was going on, but when we left there with nothing, Little Bigger Man told us to drive him somewhere else. He wasn't the kind of man that you could just leave either, so we dropped him to the next yard, then when he got out and disappeared, The General told me,

'Come let's bounce.' *Duppy truly knew who to frighten.* The General didn't like when he wasn't in control. So, we headed back to the ends. Along the way he decided to pass through Broadwater Farm. We had a look around and saw some guys. The way they greeted him, it's like they were cool, only to find out he had robbed them a few days before. He was still a different kind of guy, even though I'd seen a different face with Little Bigger Man and now I knew he wasn't totally crazy. I think he realised that I noticed and he wanted his full 100% rating back from me, so the next day we hit the road again.

This time, The General said, 'let's go Brixton.' Apparently, one man had tried to work brain on him, so I'm thinking Im going to back him in beef. When we got there, the yard man was no where to be seen so he decided, as were here, we might as well eat someone else. We saw this guy walking towards us so The General started talking to him about food(drugs). *In the late 80's Coldharbour Lane in Brixton was a serious place.* This was where we were.

The General ended up working brain on him, made him so

comfortable he got in the car, then we robbed him and sent him on his way before we drove off. As we were rolling back to the ends, something didn't feel right though. It felt like we were being followed and we were. A few miles up the road, the police pulled us. These boy dem moved a little different, like they were more angry with us than happy to be making the arrest. I thought it was strange, but didn't think to much of it as they took us in. Because of the nature of the crime and who we were, we got no bail, Court in the morning. Where with not much said, our case was dismissed. *It turned out that the yardie we robbed was working for them police.* He had licence to shot food (sell drugs) and carry weapons. The problem for the bent police was, they were being observed by other police, so when it went to court, they had to drop the charges and sweep it under the carpet, so it didn't make an even bigger mess. *That operation was bigger than I knew at the time and it would come back to haunt me.*

With us bussing that case, The General thought we were untouchable and a few days later he decided that we were going on another mission, so we rolled out. Me, The General and the Pitbull that he constantly abused, heading out of town. It was decided with a simple, let's go country. *Worse mistake of my life*!!!

I didn't know where that was, but we had a quarter of ash and a full tank of petrol as we hit the motorway. As we rolled out I asked him where we going and this is when he said Liverpool. I'd never been to Liverpool before, so when I got there and heard these people talk, I thought we was in a different country. He had these Liverpool chicks ready for us so we ended up at their yard. They were getting ready to hit one club, so we left them getting ready and went to go do a quick robbery. *Window shopping in Anfield.*

1988

I saw this big chaps in a jewellery shop that I was on so I'm thinking, yeah we gonna do this because I want that. As I'm thinking about that, The General starts talking to one man. The way they were talking, I assumed they knew each other, then The General told me we're leaving this jewellery shop robbery.

'Come let's go back to the car' he said with this new Liverpool guy. I didn't know where we going, but I'm not saying anything, I'm just along for the ride. It wasn't long before we got to this guy's yard, where he jumped out. We left him there and headed back to the girls' yard to pick them up, then we headed back to the guy's yard. The plan was, we were going to pick up a ting, then go with the girls to the club. I didn't know what they had set up, so we got back to the yard and The General tells me, 'go in there and get the drugs.' *Them man are pussy*. I thought, no problem so I put on my serious face. My scar was still fresh so I'm looking a little menacing as I walked in.

In this trap house, I hear this guy talking on the phone and say in his thick Liverpool accent, 'NOW OK,' then he put down the phone. I didn't know what that was about, and I didn't think anything of it. I walked into the front room where he was sitting down and said,

'Yeah, where's the drugs?'

I picked up the borer that he had on his dining room table. I could see he was a little nervous, so I played on it. As the guy I was talking to started getting the drugs ready, I heard one guy come into the house, but he went straight into the kitchen. I caught a brief look, but I kept doing what I was doing. I heard a few more guys come in and go straight to the kitchen too, so I angled myself in a way where I could see what was going on. The guy was taking long as more people came in. After a few more minutes he gave up the ting and I moved off to leave the yard. I've come out and seen The General with his pitbull posted up waiting for me and headed straight to the car; where the girls were in the back waiting. As The General saw me he got back into the car, ready to roll out, but then we see about 15 man charging out of the yard towards us, holding all sorts of serious weapons from machetes to axes and swords. I even saw a bow and arrow up in that arsenal.

Basically, they were holding every serious weapon you could imagine that wouldn't make noise to use. They got to the car and started SCREAMING at The General,
'WHERE THE FUCK ARE THE DRUGS, GIVE US THE FUCKING DRUGS OR WE GOING TO FUCKING KILL YA.' It was straight mayhem and chaos. Even the dog didn't want none of this one. The girls were in the back screaming their heads off.

'WE DON'T WANT TO DIE, give 'em it back.'
But me and The General are acting cool. Heart beating like wow, but no one can see that. The General got out of the car to talk and calm them down.

'WHERE THE FUCK ARE THE DRUGS?' they're screaming.

The General said, 'Don't watch nothing lads, he's a little crazy. WHERE THE FUCKS THE DRUGS YANKS?, looking at me.
All of them raced round to the passenger side door shouting and going crazy.

'WE'RE GOING TO FUCKING KILL ALL OF YA, ROB US WILL YA?.' It was a lot so I threw the thing out the window like it was wet soap. *He knew what time it was so he had called his boys to come on the phone as I went in.* They picked it up and calmed down.

As they moved away from the car we drove off. As we were driving The General said,

'That was a little close still, but at least you've still got the ting.' with his trade mark Frank Bruno laugh.

I said, 'No, are you crazy, I don't still have the ting, you don't see they was about to kill us, all of us including the dog and you asking if I've still got the ting.'

The General went ape shit, 'HOW YOU GONNA GIVE THEM PUSSIES BACK THE TING AFTER YOU'VE ROBBED THEM.'

Chapter 6

After that we dropped the girls off and decided we gonna head to Manchester's Moss Side, to try a ting there. We got there after a little while and went straight to the front line, where we saw these two black brea's shotting weed. The General instantly got into zone and said,

'Yo, you cool? My cousin's over from Brooklyn and he wants some weed.' I'm just there with my screw face not saying nothing. 'We really looking a key, you know the Yanks and their blunts, but we gonna take an ounce sample for now, to test it with a few blunts and come back for the big ting in a few.' The way The General was convincing, he even half convinced me. The guys went for it hook, line and sinker and before I knew it, we were going down the road with them to get this ounce of weed, paying absolutely nothing. The General did this from he left his front door every day, so when it came to these country areas off the ends, it was like a walk in the park for him. *He was at his best where no one knew him.* We got it, took it and left, but decided about 20 minutes later that it was so easy we should go back and get some more, before we roll out. So we did and got another ounce. It worked but when we went back it got serious, these guys were slower than us, but they weren't dickheads.

They showed us the nine millies and said, 'If you're lying, when we catch you, we going to light you up.' The General quickly dismissed any talk of bumping man with, 'Lads, none of that talk. We gonna be right back.' I could see it in their eye, that if they really believed we were bumping them, they would have moved to us, so after we got them for the second ounce we decided it made sense we get the fuck out of there, so we left Moss side and jumped back on the motorway towards Nottingham.

When we reached, guess where we went, their frontline and found two black chicks showing us love. We were looking for more victims, but because these chicks were feeling us so much, they talked us into going back to their house, where we held a fresh, then fucked til we slept. In between enjoying and selling some of that weed we stole. These chicks were local Nottingham chicks, so when they put out the word that some London man was on the ends selling weed. All the local bad boys turned up. Some of them even had eyes on our ting, but when they saw how we moved, they decided not to try it. But I could see the play because it's the same thing we did. They just knew if they tried, it wasn't going to be easy and it would have made a mess. The chicks were even in the process of washing our dirty clothes. We fucked them for a few more days, before we decided to roll out back to the ends.

In the little week we spent up North, we did a lot, more than that and even The General saw we were pushing our luck. It had been emotional and as we got back into more familiar surroundings we were both relieved, like *fucking hell we made it back* and to celebrate before going home we decided to party and headed down to Loughton; one club called Oscars. But the bouncers took one look at us and decided they weren't letting us in. *After everything we'd been through, we were going into that club whether they liked it or not.* It was like a Mexican stand-off, on top of the fact the bouncers didn't want to let us in, we didn't want to pay. Serious face to serious face, we stood there talking to them trying to convince them that they needed us in that club. We told them we weren't trouble makers; all we were looking was some gal to fuck. So after a little while with them realising we weren't going anywhere and us seeing they really didn't want us in there, we decided to pay them something. £5 for both of us, which was a bargain because it was £10 each and they let us in, where we popped off a few bottle! *Girls were all over us and it was an alright end to the adventure.*

When the party done I went home to Chingford Hall Estate. The Generals drove off and I got down on my knees and kissed the ground of Chingford Hall Estate because there were times in that mission. I actually believed I was not going to see my children again.

After that, I stopped rolling with The General. That cocaine life was long, so I went back to rolling with his Brother.

In Hindsight

With all the madness I was keeping up, it wasn't long before my Missus said she didn't want to be with me anymore. In hindsight I couldn't blame her, but at the time she was all I had, so I didn't want to let her go and I definitely wasn't moving out of the yard. I wasn't trying to make things difficult, but this was my family and I might have had some fucked-up ways, but who didn't. I guess I was just doing what I had seen my Daddy do. Anyway, I was there for a few weeks trying to win her back, but she wasn't having it.

Valentine's Day and I bought her Roses, wine and a card. I pulled out all the stops for her and she still wasn't having it, so I left the yard pissed! As I walked down the corridor to leave the building, I see this neighbour I had beef with. He kissed his teeth and gave me a look like I was the shit on the bottom of his shoe. It was the wrong time, me being so emotionally charged, so I moved to him. I'm punching him up in his face, but he wasn't having it so we were making a bag of noise in the scuffle; he was fighting me back hard. We banging neighbours walls. I can't take it away from this guy, he could scuff and as the fight went on, he started getting the better of me, so I pulled out my borer and poked him up. Some neighbours had opened their doors to see what was going on, some must have been too scared. But I know everyone could hear us because we were going at it. I thought about poking him in his neck, just dunning his dance right there (killing him) but too many people were watching, so I decided to just poke him up in his back. Blood stained his jean jacket as he screamed out in pain before I left the scene, happy with the work I'd done. I casually kept it moving, even deciding to rave that night down by Shanola's on Waterden Road in Hackney, trying to find me a new girl.

While I'm over in Hackney enjoying myself, this guy that I bored up went to my girl's house and said, 'I've got Tottenham man coming to do him something.' Obviously, I didn't care and I was going to make sure I was around, so whoever wanted to do me something could. But what he didn't tell my baby mother was, he had also told the police, so they had a warrant out for my arrest.

When I got back from the dance, I was chilling at a safe house talking to one of my bredrins about a job he was thinking about doing in Manchester. It was a cold early morning, raining and windy and we were smoking crack, getting high while we talked. Since that first time with The General, I had smoked it a few times and you could say, I had the taste for it now and because I wasn't piping it, in my mind I was ok. *I didn't do it often.* It was just a one shit spliff I thought, as we called it.

Anyway, as we chilling, out of nowhere I hear pounding on the door. This knocking didn't sound right, it was early in the morning and obviously I know what I've done so I went to see who it was. My bredrin whose yard it was had her babies around, the banging woke them up and I saw them and wondered what they thought watching a bag of bad man do their thing. Drugs being used, bad man in and out and more ripple effects we're dealing with. *If all these yutes saw was bad man in and out, police knocking the door looking for people, what were these yutes going to be.* As I got to the door, all I saw was a white man's face pushed up against the glass looking in hard. I knew that was boy dem so I made a run for it out the back. The children are watching, but I wasn't thinking about the bad example I was setting them. I went out into the garden and saw four policemen jumping over the fence, all with smiles on their face, talking about, 'Ha ha we've got you now.' Like they were hunting a wild animal! They arrested me in front of everyone including the kids and took me to jail on a Section 18, GBH.

Back To Jail (1989)

My first night in jail on this bird I reflected on what it really meant for me right now, me doing this first real bird. First they caged me in Brixton for 5 months on remand. I was used to jail all now, the jingle of the screws keys as you heard them walking up and down. The stone magnolia walls and thick metal doors. All the little birds (jail time) *I'd done so far had prepared me for this.* I knew I was looking at a few years, my longest bird so far. It was winter, so it was freezing outside and these screws had turned off the heating. They justified this by simply calling us criminals.

They would say things like, 'You don't expect us to keep you warm do ya?' "YES!" Considering you took us from our warm climates where we were minding our business, tortured, murdered and raped us and all now with this prison system; you were still able to use us as slaves. The 5 months dragged as I waited for my court date and when the day finally came.... To cut the long ting, I pleaded guilty to try reduce my sentence. They always tried to unsettle us, so they moved the goal posts. When they sent me back to the cells and the meat wagon came for me, they took me Wandsworth. They had me there for a few more months while they decided on my sentence. I spoke to my girl and she decided to come and see me so we could talk, so I sent her a VO (Visiting Order). *I remember it like it was yesterday, her bringing my daughter on the visit.* When I left my princess on road she couldn't walk, but now she was walking and looking pretty in her little pink dress.

Getting down to business though, my baby mother smiled in my face while she told me, 'We ain't getting back together. Man and man are all over me and you're in jail. Why should I wait for you? I don't like how you move and man on road are out here trying to do for me what you're supposed to. Me and you are done.' Simple like that, it was emotional and I was powerless. That was the first slap in the face, then on my birthday they sent me to Snaresbrook Crown Court, where they gave me an extra 2 years 4 months to run concurrent on my 4 year sentence, for some other robbery they had found me guilty of. (HAPPY BIRTHDAY).

I was still in that dream world and this sentence meant nothing to me, I felt like when I touched road, man dem would have to respect me now differently, all this "work" I was putting in. *How very stupid I was*! The day after sentencing they took me from Wandsworth to Camp Hill. This is the bird jail now for the young big man dem, no remand ting. The nervous and apprehensive ting wasn't there because it wasn't new to me now. I just wanted to see my surroundings and get my head down, so I could get through it as quick as possible.

The first night I arrived it was late and I was tired, so I just slept if off. In the morning when they unlocked us, I had a look to see if there was any man dem from the ends with me. First man I saw was Steplight, then Tenda and Pugglefoot, some yard man from, Tottenham, Hackney and Bow. I had met them man in other jails and any time I found the yard man circle, that was my circle in jail. On a weekend we would enjoy Jamaican dinners together. That little bit of cooking we did made us feel like we were home a little piece. But day to day bang up was bang up. Morning time the door would open at 8am. You better not still be sleeping, or you might get moved too. It was time for you to leave or almost be ready to leave to go work. They would give you half an hour to get to work, whatever slavery they had you thankful you were doing. They never gave you the best slavery position straight away either, so you had to work your way up the bullshit, imagine. I got put on a work shop first to learn wielding, it was a City and Guilds ting. That was alright, but they made sure you never forgot you were in jail.

Visits for example were always a killer. Your people would come and see you and it would be good while they were there, then the screws would tell you,

'You've got 5 minutes.' Now it's a rush ting, then it was time for them to leave. The look backs, you know with every step they take now they getting a step closer to the real world and with every step you take, you're going back to the shit hole and funny I mentioned shit. It was normal for man to put on surgical gloves for certain man that came back from their visit. If man knew a man was expecting a package, if he was weak he was getting held up in the jail toilets where man would make him wait till he shit the drugs out. Horrible! Beef and all sorts would start from that because drugs is big business in jail.

Being around man all the time was a next problem. You would catch yourself finding screws that you wouldn't look at on road attractive, man would miss woman so much. *It isn't a healthy place to be, trust me.* So, after about 18 months when my first home leave was coming up, I was well excited. I had seen bare man go off for the weekend and come back gassed. Finally the day came when it was my turn. I left out early and made my way back to the ends. Ferry to Portsmouth then train all the way to Walthamstow, then the bus back to my mums. I'd only been away just under 3 years and I was surprised with the big changes I was seeing. When you go to jail, you think life on the outside stops for you and when you touch road again the world restarts. *It doesn't, you have to catch up.* Some people can't cope with the change and reoffend on purpose to go back. I was shocked because even my little brother was on road now, going on with tings. He had a driver and now he was taking me out. That weekend he gave me my first E as we travelled to this dance called Dungeons, just off Lea bridge road. It took about 5 minutes before this feeling of tingling up and down my neck kicked in, dam it felt good. It was a Love Dove and I remember going round this roundabout feeling like I was on a fairground ride. We got in this dance and the first thing I see is strobe lights, followed by fast dancing and a bag of gal. I was on my A game after the rush from the E.

My brother took me to a little dark room and told me 'wait here' with a few blond tight little arses, keeping me company. A few minutes later, he come back with speed and weed. You could definitely say I had a good night, but the headache in the morning wasn't worth it. The side effects fucked me up big time, but I charged it to the game, it was a party and I only had a weekend, so I thought fuck it and that was just the start. My brother showed me he was grown that weekend. The Saturday night it was Warehouse a next acid rave, more drugs and gal again. That whole weekend was fire, but it went so quick, I was pissed when I had to go back.

I spent about another 3 months in Camp Hill, then they shipped me out to Down View Prison which was a bit better. It was still bang up, but with a little more freedom. They let you out more, so you could roam relatively free, but I still couldn't wait to go home. On my next home leave I decided I wasn't linking my younger brother to rave again. I just saw my children and took things easy. *Time was passing me by in jail and I was missing my children grow*. THE JAIL TING WAS LONG! All the man dem I was thinking would be giving me ratings for putting in "work" DID NOT CARE. When I was out of sight, I was out of mind. Life went on but my family who cared and were really important, were left missing me. Going back to jail this time really irritated me. It felt like the days dragged longer as my next home visit got closer because after that one, I knew it was only weeks left before my release date.

My home visit finally came and it was all about family. I went from my mum's to my grandparent's, then to my children. I didn't really want to see anyone until I touched road, so I just enjoyed some home cooked food and chilled. I was looking forward to my new life on road after jail, trust me. I was planning to go legit and the full 100, with my new welding qualification and I wanted to be a good role model for my children. I was even feeling like when I got my shit together, I was going to be able to get my baby mother back. So after that home leave, I counted down the days until it was finally the day of my release. I left jail that morning feeling real, it didn't matter it was raining outside. I saw it like the first day of my new life. I ended up doing two years eight months and 17 days, I counted them all. I came out Halloween 1991. One of my bredrins picked me up from Portsmouth and we rolled back to the ends.

We were in the 90's era now. I had left in the 80's and even though I wasn't gone for long, it was rare groove and ragga raves when I left but now it was acid and jungle raves. The difference was, in the 80's the scene was weed and alcohol, but now it was hard drugs and champs. I had trouble adapting because now everyone was dancing differently, it was all the hard drugs. They unsettled me further by putting me into a hostel in Streatham where I didn't know anyone, so every day I would leave there in the morning and go back to the ends.

When I got out of jail, I linked up with one of my bredrin's Ninja, doing my just out of jail rounds. He was dealing with a long-time friend of mine called Vanette. *He didn't even know I knew her.* Vanette was rolling with a girl called Kerry and for some reason Vanette thought me and Kerry would suit, so she linked us up. *Kerry was a boss with a bad habit.* From she hit the road, every day it was straight money she was making. Robberies and pick pocketing was her thing. Everyone from prostitutes to drug dealers and fraudsters would all roll with her because everyone around her ate. She did not mind. We linked for the first time at Snaresbrook Crown Court. That should tell you she was about this life, straight Gansta and I should have run for the hills, but I didn't. I walked into court and saw her in the dock. When court adjourned for a few minutes, she watched me for a second then said, 'Where's my kiss then, ain't you gonna kiss me?' So, I put it on her. When court reconvened, they sent her away again, but only for another 2 weeks.

When she came out they put her in a hostel in Highbury and Islington and that was us. But from she touched road, I abandoned my hostel and my hopes of turning legit. She made the dough and I was like her financial adviser. *It was a match made in the ghetto.* We would wake up a morning time, eat a food then catch a cab. Every day a different spot, but we were always heading to a shopping centre. All she needed was a crowd of people. It started off with her telling me, 'Wait here babes!' She would leave me in the cab talking to the cabby. About 20 minutes later she'd be back with about 3 purses.

I asked her the first time, 'How you come back with 3 purses, not even just one.'

She said, 'You think I've got time for the long ting. I'll rob one and stay on site. I'll leave out with about 3 then move to the next spot.' From that first day I thought, I'm rolling with her. She came back with about 9 purses, money, credit cards, all of that and she didn't mind going into banks as whoever the women on the cards were, to get that extra. She was earning from morning to night and when we went to all the hot spots, all the top man dem in se-

From The Plantation To The Streets

rious ends would fight each other to get in the cab with her. Even the cab man wasn't listening to his dispatcher when she was in the cab, they would see the money she was coming back with and just want to roll. Every day it was a mission for the love of her bad habit, the hard food, (crack) and when we finished for the day, or she felt like she had made enough, we would head down to a front line, either Sandringham or Amhurst Road der in Hackney, where they were serving it up.

This girl was 7 years younger than me, but let me be clear when I say, 'I did not influence her in no way, shape or form.' She was bringing me back to the crack life I really didn't want to live, especially as a user. If anything, I would have sold it, but being so close to someone who had the habit she had, was only going to end in a mess. I should have walked away. I tried to tell her leave it alone, but I couldn't tell her that. I could tell her other things, but she was addicted to that in a way that made me know, if I'm rolling with her I'm rolling with that and at that point in my life, I actually needed her. She made life easy for me and after trying to encourage her to leave it alone and stop throwing money away on it, I decided to take a little bit myself with her. Remember, I hadn't taken any crack since just before I went back to jail and when I got out I had seen The General. He had even given me his number, but because I didn't want to get back into any madness with him, I took it but had put his number is the bin as soon as I left him. But after I took that bit of crack with her, I was back on it. She couldn't do it any more without giving me some now and that's where my new problems started.

Now I was on it as well we needed more. It quickly got to the stage where we would spend about a grand a day on it. Then obviously we were having to live and look fresh. *Road got serious.* Life was exciting with her and we worked well together and in between the crime and drugs, we would fuck all over the place. It didn't take long before she became pregnant. It was winter time when she told me, so it was cold outside but that didn't stop what we were doing.

I told her, 'Babes, now you're pregnant we need to slow down on this ting. You know it's not good for the baby.' She wouldn't listen, that was the only thing I couldn't tell her anything about. It was fucked because I knew it wasn't right, but even if I stopped her when she was with me, I knew she would have just gone somewhere else to do it same way, so I ended up just leaving her. One time I even had a seizure in front of her while she was pregnant and that didn't even faze her for long.

Imagine, this is my first lick for the day. I set it up and lit the pipe. The next thing I remember, I'm on my back trying to get up. What really happened was, as I smoked that rock, it sent me up into the air where I landed on my back. From there, I was shaking as the smoke came out of my mouth. I can hear the Missus talking, but everything is black and I can't say anything or move.

She's saying, 'don't fuck about Mark, please don't die on me.' She was scared, backed up against the wall and when I came around we decided that, yeah then, we have to stop this and out of her mouth she said, 'I aint gonna smoke no more.'

It did faze her, but she wasn't fazed for long. It was about two days before she was back on it as normal. Even me, I was well and truly addicted, so it didn't take long before I was back on it with her. The ting had us, it really did.

Now some days I would work road with her. I might distract while she pickpocketed the victim and this was happening day in, day out as my baby was growing inside my Missus. It was madness how our baby grew with the lifestyle we were living. We were not setting our child up with the right foundations at all. She was going to be a crack baby if we kept on like this, I knew it.

I didn't know what to do about her habit, but at least I could take some of the earning pressure off of her. I didn't want her doing all the work, especially while she was pregnant so one afternoon me and one man decided we gonna do a move. It was mid day, children in their school uniforms, parents pushing prams, buses all about. A Securicor van parked up on an in and out one, by a bank. We were armed but decided that if we didn't need to use it, we wouldn't. As we approached him, the guy I was with just close lined him. The box flew out his hand. I grabbed it and we were off. We ran to the car where I was supposed to be the driver, but there was a next man in the driver's seat ready to drive, so we just jumped in and he sped off. It was madness because plain clothes police had peeped the whole ting and gave chase from the start. The driver done all kind of madness to get away endangering lives, as he drove us on the pavement. Almost crashing into people bare time, but we found our way to another alley.

Chapter 7

It was like déjá vu, police chases and alleys, but this time it was a little different. We parked up and got out with the money box, broad daylight, bag of people watching wha gwan. The police couldn't drive down the alley and follow us this time, so they gave chase on foot and we lost them. I went straight to my bredrin's yard, banging on the door but he wasn't in. He had left his bredrin in the yard with strict instructions not to let anyone in. This guy came to the door telling me, bla bla said I can't let anyone in.

I told him, 'Open the fucking door now, we just done a move, look at the box. Open the fucking door.' In the end he opened up and let us in. We were safe, even though the boy dem were still driving around the estate looking for us. Now all we were concerned with was opening that box and getting the money. We were fucking with it for a minute, then we heard the timer ting go off. We didn't want that ink to fuck up the money, so we quickly went to the bathroom and run the box under the tap. Basically we drowned the electrics, so the ink couldn't go off and spoil the money. After that we buss the ting wide open and saw twenty five bags in the box. Eight bags and some change each, nice! The biggest eat I had eaten in one go, so far and it felt real being able to give my Missus a nice three and a half bag (thousand pound) so she could calm down a little.

The driver instantly went his own way and left me and the guy I was originally going to do the move with together. First we went and done some shopping, then we went to a little hotel. But paranoia started to set in on this guy. He thought armed police were watching us and they were going to lick us down, so he started acting funny. I calmed him down that night and he linked one gal, but the paranoia was too much for me, so in the end I left him at the hotel and went about my business, to go do more shopping in Camden.

Imagine I was living so reckless, I've just done this move and I've got grands in my pocket, but I'm still teefing (stealing). I mean any shop I went into I just had to steal something, until I got to JD sports where I bought myself some Nikes. I went Mac D's after that and holla'd The General's younger brother to give him some money and buy some weed. You know support my bredrin, while I told him wha gwan. All this time the guy I did the move with was holla'ing me because we had agreed to go Cardiff, but because I didn't like how he was moving, I decided I wasn't going with him again.

A next bredrin who heard we had just buss the move told me he had a whip for sale, under 2 bags so I decided I was going to go get that, no licence and no intention of insuring the car. As long as there was a tax disc in the windscreen, in my mind I was cool. I went and got this whip (car), then I went to one crack house on the ends to get some food, but true I hadn't slept for days I was tired. I parked up outside the crack house and closed my eyes for a minute. Next thing I know I've woke up, this chick is in my passenger seat and my phone's gone. Now it's a murder ting, she's telling me from the start.

'No, it wasn't me that took it, it was yardie Merciless.'

I said 'Ok, come we go then because I don't like that pussy any way and he can get done for this now.' We got to the door. One of the drug dealers opened it and I've gone in the yard on a mad one. I put it on everyone. I'm supposed to be the "crackhead" but all these drug dealers are nervous now, furthermore I'm telling man basically,

'Either I get my phone back now, or someone's gonna dead.' Everyone was explaining and no one was chucking it so that made me know that, ok, my phone isn't here, so I ended up leaving it.

All now, the boy dem's on me and I can feel it. As I left the yard I was on my way to my Mum's when a man told me, 'your Mum's yard is getting turned upside down because of you and that robbery.' That shook me up a bit, I was thinking about that last bird I did and I didn't want to go back. So I decided fuck this, I'm flying out, back to my old stomping ground, Brooklyn.

I stayed at a safe house for a few days while I arranged my ticket, then I made my bredrin take me to the airport, checked in no problem and I was gone back to Brooklyn.

From I landed my Dad lined me up a job, working in the Coca Cola factory within the first few days. It was alright for the time being. I was there 4 or 5 days a week and it was something different to the crazy life I was living. I had moved back into my step Mum's house and I just got back to things almost like I had left them 8 years ago.

The only difference was, now I was grown the roles with me and my Dad had changed. I would get flashbacks of when I was a yute, how he used to treat me. He had been holding on to some of my money too and I wanted to know why. He had said some bullshit about I was going to spunk it (waste it), but it was my money to do what I wanted with, so I wanted it. Now as a man I was ready for him and I wished he would do something, so I could show him how much of a man I was now. Imagine, now I'm here with him, he needs to answer questions. Back in the day I had to give right answers, now he's having to give right answers. I was crossing the line with him and he was having it. It's like he knew I wanted to do him something for everything he had put me through. I would ask him what happened and why with authority in my voice. But now he was sensible all of a sudden. He wasn't the same guy and he could see, I was now a product of what he had made me, and he had a bag of regrets. He wasn't Super Man any more. I was on him for everything, like if he told me he was going to do something and he didn't, the next time I saw him I would put it on him. I'd make him uncomfortable and I could see that. He was trying to be a good Dad now, I didn't care. *It was 20 years too late.*

My Missus was supposed to come out and link me, but it didn't take me long to realise she wasn't coming. I figured she was back on the ends making that money to smoke, so I just got on with it. I would think about her though and my new baby on the way. And after about a week without hearing from her, I start wondering wha gwan. *She had gone quiet on me.*

I called my bredrin who would know in London and he told me she had got nicked (arrested) again, so right there I decided I needed to get back to London. I thought I would be able to sneak back in the same way I had snuck out. I booked my ticket and a few days later, I was arriving back at Heathrow Airport. I got off the plane and everything was nice until I got to customs, where one blond chick approached me talking about, 'Hi, can you come with me for a minute please?' I played it cool and followed her to a little room where her and a next one started interrogating me.

They told me straight, 'We stopped you because we suspect that you are trafficking drugs, so we're going to search you.' Then they patted me down and found nothing, so they decided they were going to strip search me. I was looking very fresh and on reflection, living in this racist world, you might say I fitted the profile and based on that, they needed to search me.

Even though I had nothing on me, they didn't believe it and still wanted to fuck with me so next they X-rayed me. They were begging, and they told me that the hot dog I had eaten in JFK was drugs, so they put me in a cell with toilets that were shaped in a way where they could see all the shit. Then they watched me, they even fed me Burger King, so I would shit. After the long ting, I finally let it out and they saw it was nothing, then they put a call out to all police in London to check if I had any warrants. This is when Chingford replied and told them to keep me because they were coming. These pussy holes came to me happily to tell me, 'Chingford Police said they want to talk to you, so you won't be going anywhere.' I was pissed!

Looking at the evidence they had on me, I just pleaded guilty to that, so they sent me to Pentonville while I was on remand.

The Missus had been convicted of robbery and she was in Holloway serving a 3-year sentence. I had come back to see her, so I put in an application for an inner prison visit and they gave it to me. It was good to see her even though it was only 2 hours. Her belly was getting big and it wasn't a good look, but it was the life we had chosen, and we were having to live it. After Pentonville they moved me on to Brixton for about 5 months and in that time, I got to see my youngest princess in the flesh for the first time. Her Mum managed to get another visit with me. Princess was about a month and my baby mother had given birth to her in jail. It was lovely to see her, as brief as it was but after that I didn't see her for more than a year, *at least I had that memory*.

They ended up giving me a quick 5 years. These birds were starting to add up! When they convicted me I got sent to Maidstone. Maidstone had a few killers in there still, it was a serious jail. But it was decent at the same time in the sense that at least you were able to train in whatever you liked to do. We got 2 hours a day. It even had a swimming pool. Some man would play football, but I was a gym man.

I was there for a while then Reggie Kray came in. He still had his aura even with his grey hair. He was in his 60's then and he'd been in jail 30 years already, but he had his circle and no one fucked with him. On this bird I started to see the long sentence man dem, the lifers and that. They would stay to themselves them lifers more time because it was a head fuck for them. They didn't want to talk to the man that was getting out. We used to play dominoes them times there, day in, day out. Man would gamble drugs money live in front of the crooked screws. Some man, mainly the junkies would run up mad debts, all £500 debts and act like they were going to pay, but they couldn't so they would have to go to the protection wing. Now you see them, now you don't type ting. These man would have to stay protected until they got moved off to a new jail and in that new jail hope that no one from the old jail turned up to expose a man. In my time in Maidstone, it was more time me and Ninja, a next Ninja that rolled. We both smoked weed, we were both barbers and on the gym ting, so we clicked. He was a yard man too, so we even cooked up the same Jamaican food. We were rolling like family.

The jail ting could really drive you mad though and one day after about 6 months the screws (prison warden) pissed me off. It was Weetabix day and my neighbour said I could have his milk. I told the screw serving up, but him being a wanker told me I needed to go and get my neighbour. *On the 4th floor, a bag of stairs and this guy wants me to walk up all those stairs so he can come back and say, yeah.* I even started walking, then I thought this screw's just taking the piss. NO!

I went back to the screw and told him, 'just give me the fucking milk and with a big smile on his face, like he was happy he was drawing me out, he said 'NO,' wrong move! I jumped the counter and gripped him. I grabbed a pan and did brace up to rass him with it. The other screws standing next to him saw what was going on and didn't want nothing to do with it. They just called for backup. *It was a standoff.* I'd had enough of their shit and I felt like I needed to show this pussy, but it didn't last long because some of the guys I respected came and talked me down, but I made the screws know that day, don't fuck. It felt good as well but my punishment for that was the block. They had me in there for a month and it's like they wanted to ship me out, but the meat wagon wasn't coming, so they just left me in the block to rot. All the other guys who came to the block after me, came out before me. I was subhuman to them, so they could just treat me anyhow they wanted.

In the end I did wild out like they expected me to, til one of the softer screws came and talked to me normally. As he gave me that respect, I gave him the same respect back and explained how I was feeling. Then I told him, 'if they aren't gonna move me to another jail, why not just move me to another wing, so I don't have to see that screw and that screw don't have to see me.' He took that idea back to the other screws and they thought about it then agreed, so I got moved to a next wing in the same jail.

That worked out better for me, the screws saw me as a problem and the man dem noticed me a little more, true I was coming from a month on the block. You had to do something in jail to get noticed, or you would be seen as a nobody. I wasn't making big money, so I had to be violent and make people know, I would do my ting because I needed all the piece of the pie that was mine. I was the barber as well within my prison circle, so I would get a pass to go from wing to wing, when man asked me to cut their hair. I was alright in jail tru that and I would get brought in on whatever man was on, so I ended up turning collector on the different wings. Nine times out of ten, if man had something for one of my people, when I came for it, I would collect and this is where my respect levels started to grow in jail even more. I'm in a nice place now in Maidstone, I'm smoking daily, eating well and tings is as nice as they can be for a man in jail. The screws were the problem more than anything for me. They didn't like things to be comfortable for man and moving on to the new wing this one screw, Mr Pricks, had decided based on what he had heard, that I was trouble. He wasn't trying to give me a chance, but it didn't bother me straight away. I actually even did well ignoring him for a few weeks until I noticed this thorn in my side, so I let him have it with my mouth. I realised that if I did him something, I'd go back to the block and I might be staying in the B Cat prison for longer than I had to. The B Cat regime was a little harder than the C Cat ting and I knew my C Cat was due to come soon. The C Cat would have brought me closer to my people and that's what I wanted more than anything now, especially with my youngest daughter on road. I really wanted my home leave, but because I was a flight risk, they wouldn't ok it. I forced their hand with the C cat ting though because I could see, man dem worse than me with money would pay the screws and the screws would give them a nice up report, so they would get let out. Yet I'm being told that because I flew out I can't get no home leave, blatant corruption.

In the end they gave me the transfer to a C Cat called Down View. I was alright with Down View, but within the first few weeks I got into a little something. There were a few guys doing stuff I wanted to be around because they were moving the supplies I wanted. One guy, a coolie yute had just come back from a home leave and brought in a package. I had asked him the first day he got back for some weed, but true he didn't know me he said, 'I've already sold out the ting.' He hadn't, but he wanted to release it in bits each day.

The next morning one white brea came to his cell asking to buy a ten-pound bag then robbed him for his package right there. I was in my cell and heard the commotion, so I came onto the landing to see wha gwan. When I heard I decided to back him because I knew, if I did that it would put me in a nice place with these guys. *I didn't know the coolie yute and his man dem were all pussies, so we went and found the guy.* They had all talked this ting about they were gonna do this and that, but when we got there now, it's like none of them wanted it.

The brea said straight, 'Yeah I robbed him and none of you man are getting back shit, if you try it I'll bore up every one of you and I don't care if I go hospital, I'll be back and all of you will get it.' *This guy just had a lot to say and I didn't like none of it.* I was in the back listening to this and none of them guys were saying anything, so I had to move from the back to the front. All the other guys wanted to get out of there, but I thought, I can't be having this. I asked him if he was talking to me as well and that's when he jumped up with his little homemade borer and attacked me. It was on. He was a meaty guy, but a little chubby, I was in good shape. With the first strike I managed to disarm him, but he was on it and the screws knew it was going off because they had done already heard, so we didn't have much time to do this. With every move we were trying to knock each other out. That one was about 50/50 before I had to get out of there, trying to get away without getting caught by the screws, but they caught me as I was leaving. Straight Block! I shut down the jail as they walked me through. It's true I was on the landing that smokers wasn't allowed to be, fighting with a man that was from that landing and it was over drugs. *It wasn't a good look for me as a new coming.*

While I was on the block, they offered me exercise but because I had just got to that block and I didn't know anyone. I didn't want them to see me before I got my head together and shit. The brea I had just fought took his exercise though with his face all mash up. When man asked him what happened, he said 4 man rushed him.

Blatantly lying and I could hear him, but that was the least of my worries. The next day they put us both before the governor and to make things easier, we both agreed to squash it and shook hands in front of the governor, that was it.

When they put us back on the wing, the little worm who had set it all up got exposed. He was supposed to be the coolie brea's friend, so when it all came out, man told him he better get the package back. He got scared and went to the screws and before you knew it, they were pointing the finger at me assuming I'm gonna cause more trouble, so I got shipped out that day, only across the road but back to an A and B Cat jail. High down. They held me there for a few weeks, while they decided where to send me for my next 18 months behind bars. That ended up being Coldingly. Thankfully another C Cat jail. This jail was a working man jail. It had a metals shop there where people would make things like number plates and stop signs. There was so much metal around, as you can imagine, the amount of weapons that came out of there was crazy. Man would make a mad weapon, smuggle it back to the wing then sell it just in case man wanted to get dark, if the time to get dark ever came. Obviously, if you got caught, you were going back to an A or B Cat prison and your sentence would get extended, so it was a regression ting. I stayed in Coldingly for about 9 months and in that time, I bucked up with my friend V's baby father, the one who had linked me with Kerry my second baby mother. It was crazy because when I left V on road, she didn't have no baby. Now I'm meeting her new baby father in jail. Me and him started rolling from then and on his next visit with her, I tagged along and said, 'Hi,' before leaving them to talk. Nothing really major happened in Coldingly and I just did my time in peace, before I was then transferred to The Mount, Hemel Hampstead. This was a jail that made me know I was closer to home. A lot of London man were in this jail and it made me, what they call jail happy! As the days to my release got closer, I had trouble sleeping, so my time started to drag. I was so fit at the time I had trouble tiring myself out. Clock watching and all that made it long, but then they transferred me again to

Blunderston. I didn't care where they wanted to send me by now because I was getting out soon. In that 3 months in Blunderston, I just trained cardio and got myself ready for road. *I got through it finally and it was the day of my release.*

Chapter 8

They gave me my travel warrant, my discharge money but no address to go to, not even a hostel. The weather was always raining and cold when I touched road, but I was out. That was sunshine right there so I didn't care. I didn't know what I was coming out to though. My ride or die chick had fucked off. She had got out 18 months before me and she hadn't come to see me. She had gone right back to the drugs and back to that life, so when I got out I decided I was going to do me. It was obvious she was doing her, so I thought fuck it then.

Imagine now the shame of having to eat humble pie and ask my first baby mother if she would put me up in her yard, until I sorted something out. She had a new man with a new yute. The system had failed me all now. How could they be letting me out without finding me a hostel that I could go to. It wasn't like they didn't have enough time to sort one out for me. I had to ask her and she kind of had to accept, for the sake of the children. I felt like a waste man, the lowest because I wasn't supposed to need to ask those favours from my baby mother and imagine how my yutes would have been looking at me. This fake rep I was earning on road with all this bird I was doing, wasn't all it was cracking up to be. It was lucky I had a decent relationship with my baby mother's new man. He knew all about me, so he was a little nervous at my arrival, but I was thinking about things now. I didn't want to look like the bad guy in front of my yutes and if I had done him something, it would have made things bad for me, even seeing my yutes and I would have had to come out of the house. He was a few years younger than me. He was actually my little brother's younger. On top of the fact, he was cool, so it made me not want to dark him anyway.

I'd been out a few days when he asked me to go down the road with him. I didn't have anything to do like that, so I went and we ended up at one of his bredrin's yard. As they were talking they left me in the front room for a minute, then I smelt that smell I didn't want to in the air, like a funny type of plastic burning. It was the crack and the next baby father asked me,

'Yo Yanks, you want some of this?'

I should have said "NO!"

I know but I didn't and I hit it and in that moment I got the taste for it right back. I don't know what I was thinking, licking the pipe with my baby mother's new Man. I didn't know what to do with myself while I was sitting down in my baby mother's house after that, but I didn't want to look like a waste man. My children were watching and my baby mother was watching too. After that lick of the pipe, I didn't do it with him again. I went and linked other guys, but now because I had that taste back, it started taking up my time. This went on for a few weeks but when I saw what was happening, I decided I had to get out of my baby mother's house, so she couldn't see me fucking up as well. It took about 8 weeks, but I finally got my own place, so at least I could fuck up my life without her seeing.

How could I really be comfortable seeing my baby mother cool and living good with a next man. That could have even played a part in me starting to smoke again, subconsciously. The only plus I could see at the time was, I still had some money from my last robbery, so when one of my youngers asked me to go into business with him and open a barber shop, I was on it. I put some money down and that was me. I wanted to do the right thing now. I know I had started smoking again, but I still wanted to set a good examples for my children and I definitely didn't want to go back to jail.

I got some flyers printed and I hit the road promoting the new barber shop. Every day I was up and down Walthamstow Market chatting to people and making connections with potential clients. Cutting hair in between to break up the day. The market was lively, so it was a good time.

I saw my youngest's baby mother in the market too around the time. We saw each other same time, but she tried to duck me, probably thinking I was going to beat her up for not coming to see me when I was in jail. I pulled her up anyway and told her, 'don't watch that, I understand why you didn't look for me. If you need support or anything holla me.' I gave her the address to my new place and left her to do her thing; still robberies and theft.

Me and my new business partner started having problems soon after we went into business with each other because he was a born-again Christian now. I remembered him before that, when he was one of my youngers in the back ground. He was on the ting back then, but now when I want to put on my Tupac and Biggie rap shit, he wants to talk to me like we can't play that music in here. With alittle bit of tones. It hurt my feelings still so after a while, I said 'Look, just give me my money back and I'll leave you to it.'

He said, 'cool', so we agreed to part ways. I took my money back and kept it moving, so now I'm back on road. A few days after leaving the barber shop I saw The General. He asked me why I hadn't holla'd him and told me that money was making and I should roll. I weren't on nothing that he was on, but I didn't tell him that. I just explained that I had been in jail and now I was back I would holla, so he gave me his number again and again when I left him, I put his number in the bin. I was trying and rolling with The General, sooner or later I knew I would either be going back to jail or something else. *Neither options I wanted.*

Marky B

Lights Camera Action

All now I'm living in Leytonstone, Cathall Estate. Man like Marky B aka Mark Gamble came back into my life. He was a party man like myself and we had got to know a lot of the MC's and DJ's of the time, in the garage scene. A lot of the time we would be behind the DJ booth, so when we touched the dance floor, I was like one of the DJ's or MC's and a bag of gal would jump on me. I can actually say, I was addicted to raving and the life that came with it. Fuck, fuck, fuck, that's all these girls wanted from me. Sometimes I'd link a gal and she would have me locked up in her bed room for 2, 3 days. *Not even kitchen I did see*. After a while I would just take them back to my yard because at least I knew then, that I'll be eating when I need to, instead of them just taking my energy and not giving anything back.

It's true now I was back to having time on my hands, it didn't take long before I was back on the stuff. I buss one move and got a quick 3 bags for it. Now I had a little money in my pocket that had come in relatively easy I decided, let me go get me some food and smoke a little ting. Up until then I had been smoking, but only when I was around smokers and I was smoking their ting, but when I buss that move and bought my own ting something changed.

Bad Mistake!

I got a little £50 ting and that was done in a few hours, but I enjoyed it and chilled off. I was meeting a bag of gal because of all the raves and I was fucking a lot because I had my yard. It was 1996 and this was the best year of my life. Me and Marky B were rolling and we even got a job together, working in Hackney off Mare street. Them times der, we were on fire. I was the dark skinned one and Marky B was the light skinned one. We were cleaning up round there with the gal and man dem loved us for how we were moving. We would work that hair cutting ting during the day, then go home, eat a food, freshen up and change ready to hit the clubs.

I remember we went West End often. This one night Marky said, 'it would be good if we found two gal driving.' So said, so done, we ain't been walking more than 5 minutes when we find two gal, decent tings as well and after a little small talk they said, 'So where we going?' We didn't mind. One of them suggested a club called Samantha's. I hadn't been there before, so we said, 'Fuck it, Samantha's it is then' and headed there. When we got there, I saw one tick (well-shaped) chick outside that caught my eye. The girls we were with went ahead of us, paid and went in. I had a track suit on, so the bouncers decided to give me trouble and talk about I can't come in. Mark had two shirts on, so he took one off and gave it to me, I changed right in front of them but they still gave me a little problem. In passing I had said to the chick I had taken a liking to, 'You're fit you know' and she had put it on me loud, like 'WHAT DID YOU SAY?' I backed it and said again louder 'YOU'RE FIT YOU KNOW!' She took a liking to me from that and decided to help me get in. The bouncers let us in after the chick put her little word in, so now we in this club. The original girls that we had come with were in there, but they didn't like how this new chick with us was moving. She was too rowdy for them. So they decided that they wanted to leave. Marky was on one of them, so he was trying to leave with them. But, I liked this tick one. I was trying to hang with her. Marky was telling the other two gal to stay, but they weren't on it and they were telling Mark to tell me to come. I was staying where I was. After a while them two chicks left and Marky stayed with me. We were in the dance now with this buff ting. She told me as I was admiring her, 'I stopped with the steroids about 4 months ago' and that just interested me even more.

We stayed at Samantha's til about 2 that morning, then we decided to leave to go back to my buff ting's yard. We jumped in a black cab heading to Islington. *This chick was rowdy, I liked it.* She even bad up Marky for a minute with a quick, 'You better shut the fuck up or I'll lick out your teet.' But it was all a little banter (joke) still. When we got to her yard we made ourselves comfortable as she went to the kitchen to fix us some drinks and came out with the drinks and a pet Iguana; then put it on my lap and asked me if I was scared?

I said 'NO,' but I kind of was still. *You know them funny animals man ain't familiar with.* We were getting on well though, giggling and shit. I asked her where the toilet was on a little wink, wink and she personally directed me upstairs, where she was waiting for me when I came out. Then she took me to her bedroom, where we had a quick beat (fuck). All this time Marky was downstairs trying it on with one lesbian ting that weren't having it. When we finished our first beat and went back downstairs my one said, 'Boy we shouldn't have done that you know. If my man had come back and caught us, he would have killed everybody.' *Apparently, he was some bad man*, but I had already decided that I'm trying to fuck again if she lets off and if her bad man boyfriend comes while I'm fucking, I'm fighting for my life and getting out of there. We went upstairs again a few hours later and beat (fucked) again, then she forced the issue, so we left after she gave us some weed.

I remember Marky didn't really want to go out that night, but we had a good night and he became my raving partner. He would talk to me about smoking my shit spliffs in the dance though, that was the only thing he didn't like. I used to stink out the place with shit (crack) spliffs and he would always say.

'Yanks man, you shouldn't smoke that shit.'

But I didn't care. I smoked crack on a bad man ting and I felt like this made me look like a bad man in the raves. It was that type of circle we were in, where I would meet bare man who was on it as well, who were surprised at the fact that I was on it because I looked so fresh. It's like this attracted certain man to me because it was generally thought that if you were on crack, you would look a certain way, but I didn't so man was drawn to me because of that. This lifestyle went on, straight raving all weekend and smoking crack for about six months. Then Marky got his girl pregnant, so that kind of rocked me a little bit as it was us in the club before, but it turned to just me.

In this drug infused party lifestyle, I linked a next chick who was addicted to Charlie (cocaine). We met in the club and instantly got on well. I took her back to my yard and we fucked, then we started linking. But this chick was on the Charlie hard. Every time she came, she would either bring Charlie, or want to get Charlie, so we would both go down to my link and get it. This chick was well to do. Her pups was rich and she lived in Chelsea, so I would go and spend some nights over there in the nice part of town too. She had a sister who lived in Shepherd's Bush who was more of a street girl. She was selling herself to fund her drug habit, where my one, worked as a dental assistant to support hers.

True I knew what she was like, I decided to bring my drug dealer bredrin to her yard to work with the sister. I figured if he comes with me, we would save some P, but now the drug dealer was with us, it's like something changed in my one. After we beat we had a silly argument, so I decided I was bouncing. But my drug dealer bredrin wasn't ready to bounce yet. I left him there with the two gal. I think he ended up beating both of them, but it was minor. I just called a man to come pick me up and went back to the ends. It was all the same again, it was a dirty cycle and my wind down from this silly argument was to go get some food and smoke it, all on my own. *Making a bad situation even worse.*

This would go on week in week out, but what's making this worse now is, my bredrins who smoke are smoking in my yard. Obviously, they would be bringing me in and we would be smoking together, but now when they leaving to go do moves to get more, I'm going with them because I want more as well. At first, I was just the lookout. Man would go do their jobs and come back with tings. They knew who to sell the goods they stole to, so they could tell me anything and give me what they wanted. But as time went on, I got to know what they were stealing and how much it was worth. Along with who bought these things, so it didn't take long before I was out there doing the moves myself, eating all the money myself too. It was easy and the money was quick and decent if you did enough, along with obviously eating all the man dem on road that I didn't like. I was eating every day from crime on road and that was feeding a crack habit that was getting worse.

Now, I had linked my newest ting who was an accountant. She loved to party and that's how we had linked. She was with someone, but she didn't care. He didn't like to rave and I did, so I was like her raving boyfriend. The first time she came to my yard, we were there chilling, then I heard my letter box go like someone was there. I wondered and crept to my door to see my drug addict baby mother standing there. I was like, *what the fuck is she doing here*, but remembered I had told her on road in the market that if she needed any support to check me. I opened the door and told her, 'I've got a gal in my bedroom.'

She said, 'I've got the ting and it's cool, I will go in the front room.' A brea had actually brought her to my yard and she had told him to wait. Anyway she came in and went to the front room where she started building the ting. I went to the bed room and told my new ting that my baby mother had turned up and she wasn't 100% cool. The chick told me she wasn't going to stay because she wasn't looking to fuck on that first night anyway, but she didn't want to make it seem like she was being rushed out the yard, so she stayed for a bit. I went back into the front room and saw my baby mother piping the ting right there. I built a crack spliff and took it to my new ting in the bedroom. I knew she was on the cocaine and she took pills, so she was a druggy, but I didn't know she was on the crack too until I gave her a spliff and she smoked it all down to nothing. She didn't even give me any back. Then she told me she was bouncing, so I walked her to the cab station and she got a cab. When I got back to my yard Kerry was still there. That night me and her ended up fucking. It was the first time we had in about 3 and a half years.

I thought after that, me and her were going to get back together like the old days because that's how it had started. Her stealing, me watching her back til we'd made enough money, then we'd go back to my flat to smoke. It didnt go like that though unfortunately. After a few days we went to do some shopping and when we got into a crowd of people she just vanished on me and I knew I just had to get on with my life because I had learnt, she was like that. I just had to keep doing me, day in, day out to get money for my drugs habit.

I wasn't going out like that anymore. The raving ting had burnt me out. But, as time went on, I realised that me being away from the raving scene was really causing me the problem because I wasn't on the drug so hard when I was out in the club. I decided the club scene was better than staying home with a bag of time on my hands. I got back into it and started linking some of the old faces who were still on it. *The ones who were maintaining.* I looked at that and knew that's where I wanted to be. Smoke the ting, but still look how I'm supposed to and have the respect in my circles.

So I started rolling with my drug dealer bredrins who had the club scene on smash. I didn't have to put my hand in my pocket when I was with them, coz they had guest list for everywhere. On the Saturday night we would touch The SW1 Club. After SW1 about 7 in the morning we would head on to The Chunnel Club in South. A massive queue had always formed by the time we got there, but we didn't have to wait in that. We just walked straight to the front and we were in. I was like these man's hench man, just out of jail looking in good shape, down for whatever and on the Class A. *I intrigued all the gal I came into contact with and I loved it.* From the Chunnel Club, we would go to the Boat Party on the river. We had a change of clothes in the car and it come like a marathon. It was the Tupac and Biggie days 1996. Party, party, party, so by the time 97 came around I was going Glastonbury as that's where this drugs money really was for the street man dem. When we got to Glastonbury that year I saw what time it was straight away. Guys hadn't even got in yet and money was making in the car park. We scaled the fence quickly then went to the exit to get the stamp like we had already paid. Now we could go and come as we pleased. We're making money selling dud E's laced with nail polish. Glastonbury was big enough to make a dud sale and not bump heads with the man again, but sometimes we did and we would fuck them off, or sometimes they would even buy more duds. There were enough druggies for all of us, so we would link other drug dealers doing their ting and no one had a problem. I mean everywhere we went, kilos of weed, cocaine and brown with a bag of pills. Whatever you wanted was there. Glastonbury was a real madness that year. We made a mad P. I came back and bought a bag of clothes and other shit with the money I made, then got back to my regular shit.

Chapter 9

This went on until February 98 where I got nicked for a theft. They sent me Pentonville for about 2 months, then they let me out back to do the same ting, teefing, raving, smoking, basically doing what I wanted for the whole of 98. I remember that same year I linked Kerry again. True she knew where my flat was, she would turn up from time to time. This time when she turned up, she had stopped the stealing, but even worse now, she had started selling herself, she was on the brown (heroin) now too, so she was falling to pieces, she had lost a few of her teeth and she needed help. *She was a certified junky now.*

On my constant search for my next fix, a few weeks before she turned up again, I had linked up with some guys who had brought some cocaine in from Toronto. It was about a kilo and they were using my yard as the science lab. She had turned up in the middle of this and all this cocaine around wasn't good for either of us. I had been around her while she had put in all the work for years, so now I had tings around me, I had to let her smoke too if she wanted, even though I knew I shouldn't have. She was in the bedroom while we were in the kitchen doing our ting and every now and then, I would bring her some more to smoke. She would hit some then leave it. I could only imagine what she had been through because I didn't know her to take time with crack, but she was hitting it then falling asleep.

After these guys had finished doing their ting, they left me to clean up. There was bare dust and pebbles around and this should have taken me no more than an hour, but as I was cleaning, I would burn a spliff or hit the pipe and this went on for days. It got so bad I couldn't talk, guys would come to my yard and see me fucked out my face. All I could do was point to the kitchen and they knew what time it was. I needed help as well. All this time, my baby mother was in the bed smoking when she felt like it, but because things had got so bad for her, she didn't want to be around anyone. She was with me for a few days, then when we touched road again she ditched me. She must have thought about the old days and the fact that we were in my yard keeping up with fuckery, while our yute was being brought up and looked after by her Mum in Plymouth. I was hurt she ditched me, I can't even lie. I wanted to have her back and at least try to help her, but she wouldn't let me. I just had to continue to do me. I didn't see her again for about another 9 months.

A few days after she left, she was still fresh in my mind when I saw The General. I heard his voice before I saw him and thought, shit. But, when I saw him, he had lost about half his body weight and he really didn't look well. He still had that deep aggressive voice, but he looked like the wind could blow him over now.

He said, 'Yes Yanks, wha gwan?'

I said, 'Wha gwan General, what happen to you, you don't look well?'

He said, 'I know, I'm not well, but they don't know what's wrong with me. Take my number and phone me this time Yanks.'

I said, 'Nah, General for real, I will phone you.' He looked fucked and like he needed help now. I intended to phone him this time because I could see he needed me now. He was still on the drugs and I wondered if my life was going to end up like his.

I had started linking this dentist at the time. She was living in Chelsea as well and I was driving one little Vauxhall Cavalier now. I would travel from my place in Leytonstone to Chelsea to check her. This chick was alright, I had met her in one after party in Tottenham. She was on the cocaine and pills, but she had it under control. Our relationship was a weekend type situation for her. Me and her weren't serious like that, but if I saw her in a dance, no matter who she was talking to, when I told her we bouncing, she was coming and that was it. This was how it was and I liked it like that. I didn't want any commitment at the time, I was just on my own ting in a daze.

I had phoned The General a few days after I saw him and he told me he had gone to hospital, but he didn't like what they were going on with, so he had checked himself out and gone home. A few days after we spoke, he died, leaving his Missus and yute. That hit me hard because even though he was on too much madness for me, he was still my bredrin. The funeral came shortly after and I was one of his pallbearers. It was a very emotional day for the people that came out for him and people had all kinds of ideas on how he had died. Some man thought he had been poisoned with arsenic, by some of the drug dealers he used to rob.

Life was a mess all now and I was using girls as my stress reliever. I had a bredrin who had been talking to this chick I used to beat and guess where she was, in jail. She would write him letters, but true he wasn't feeling her anymore, he would give me the letters to read. She was coming out of jail soon and she was good for another fuck. I decided I was going to pick her up on her release date. But, it's only as I waited for her and linked a guy I knew from Camp Hill jail. He told me he was waiting for her too. It turned out, he was her boss who had her on road in King's Cross selling food. So, I was there with him waiting to see what other gal came out and who do I see? My baby mother Kerry. She was as shocked to see me as I was to see her, so she asked me

'why you outside here, who you waiting for?' I told her straight what the deal was and we just moved on. I asked her who was picking her up, but she didn't have anyone collecting her so I told her, 'My car's right there you know.' She jumped in and I brought her back to the ends. Them times there, one of my youngers crack was firing, so we went Ching Hall to get the food, then I took her back to my yard in Leytonstone to smoke. After the food done, we touched road and done some robberies to get some money, then we went and got some more food. We smoked that too then she told me she was just going shop and disappeared on me.... again.

I quickly got back to doing me. I wasn't gonna keep letting this chick come dizzy me up. *Fuck that.* I just continued what I was doing, stealing, robbing and all the other stuff in the middle to maintain my habit.

My new ting now was stealing cars, so I could taxi ravers from the rave to their yard. Imagine, I would be in a stolen car, piping crack waiting to drive a raver home. That was working too for a while, then it got bait so I ditched that idea, but I didn't ditch getting HIGH. I remember getting so high one night, I left out my yard in Leytonstone and just started walking. I walked for miles and ended up in Holborn, looking for anything to rob. Nothing was safe from me that night, it needed to be clamped down or it was coming with me. It was about 7 in the morning by the time I got to Holborn and as I was walking, I saw someone who looked like my brother. I knew he worked around Holborn, but I definitely didn't expect or want to see him. As I called out his name he turned around. I wasn't happy to see him and at that time in the morning. Especially knowing that he knew what I was on and for me to know that he had got up out of his bed, normal to start his day of WORK and we were linking up like this.

As I left my brother it was a point of realisation, I needed to come off road. What was I really doing? He's my younger brother and he's going to work and me, the older brother is on road stealing and robbing to feed a crack habit. I went home after that and thought about my life, but my soul searching didn't last long because I went back on road the same day. I was on it; I needed to get high, so I walked now in a different direction. I didn't want another surprise like linking my brother again, so I stayed localish and ended up in Walthamstow robbing one car when the owner came out and caught me.

He said, 'Oi!'

I came out slowly, turned to him and said, 'What?' He didn't want to challenge me, so I turned and started walking away. He called the police straight and as I buss the corner I was on my toes. I run through the local estate, Priory Court and ended up knocking on my bredrin's door at the other end of the estate. The police had passed me a few times on my get away. I thought I had lost them. He let me in and I went and hid in one of his cupboards. I was there for a minute, then I heard the boy dem in his yard walking up his stairs. *Fuck*! They got me out and arrested me on an idiot theft charge and took me to Edmonton Police Station. In the meat wagon, I had all these police pussy holes eye balling me. True I was pissed, I was eye balling all of them right back. I didn't like how they had me, so I was pushing out my chest on them like if you want it then, we can do this now. That was one of the reasons they gave for not giving me bail, my aggressive nature.

From Edmonton they sent me back to Pentonville. It was my sentencing day. I left Pentonville to go Waltham Forest Magistrates Court and as I was coming up the stairs, who do I see? My baby mother, Kerry. She had been sentenced to another bird, but as I went to hug her, she pulled away like she didn't want to touch me. There were some rumours going around at the time and I think that's what made her pull away. But, she hurt me with that pull away there, under the circumstances. But we talked for a minute still.

I asked her, 'How you doing?'

She said, 'cool.'

I told her, 'I'm still in the same place, come check me.' But, now we were getting moved on because I had screws with me and she had screws with her, so that was it. I went into court where they ended up giving me 5 months, then they sent me back to Pentonville. I didn't see road again for about 2 and a half months, that was a minor though, one of my shorter stays. Back on road now into my never-ending whirlwind of partying and drugs.

Smoke To Ease The Pain

That year with all that had happened, I would still say it was a good year. The club scene had been on fire for me and to put all the fuckery behind me, I ended the year at the Basildon Mansion Party. That was a massive dance still! It went on for 3 days around Christmas '98. I even bucked up my first baby mother in there, trying to catch her man out. It was crazy because all her girls were in relationships with my people and they were all trying to catch their men.

They all came asking me, 'Is he here? Have you seen him?'

I'm just saying 'Nah,' and trying to find man to give them the heads up before their Missus actually caught up with them. In the midst of all of this, I linked one next chick called Emma. As I was going back into the rave from the toilet, she was coming out of the rave looking for a toilet and we crossed paths. We shared a quick smile then started a little two step with each other. The first thing she said to me as we were dancing was, 'I've just got out of jail and I'm on bail.' It's like she was trying to impress me, but that didn't. After a few minutes she said, 'I'm just going toilet.' I waited for her and we spoke a little more, but I was stiff because my baby mother was in the dance and out of respect, I didn't like to do that. It was so bad, I actually just left her on the night.

Where my yard was so active, it didn't take long before drug dealers thought it was a good idea to start serving up outside my yard. I watched them for a few weeks, then I decided I'm robbing them. These man think it's all cool 'coz my yard's active with cats (druggies). It's not! I called them up to my door and took what they had, then closed the door. True they knew about me, they just bounced. I guess they didn't want to make any wrong move so they thought about it first, then came back a little while later knocking. I saw it was them and told the guy that was with me in my yard to go see what they want.

They said to him, 'Look all we want is the ting back, we don't want no trouble.' My guy told me, so I broke off a bit and gave them some back. They took that then bounced, I was using my name and aura to take the piss, but if I wasn't that terrorist guy, that could have easily got serious. I was living reckless and something needed to change, but I didn't know what was going to happen to make me change, so it was what it was. The days were drifting in and out as one big blur really. A few days later it was Friday again and I decided to go to a pub for karaoke night, on the Lea Bridge Road. Who do I see, that same chick I had started talking to in the Mansion Party but had left because my baby mother was there. It seemed like it was destiny for us to link. We started talking and before I knew it, she was moving into my yard and we were living together.

We were in my place for about 6 weeks and things were so good with us, I started getting feelings for her. I'd say at the time she was good for me because she didn't smoke crack and every time I did it infront of her, she would cry. This started making me feel some type of way because I could see I was hurting her. She just didn't want to see me hurt myself like this. She got so emotional about it, I actually stopped smoking it while I was around her. It was around the time my two front teeth fell out from the accident I had all those years ago. I was in Chingford Hall Estate, when a guy holla'd me to say wha gwan, the next thing I knew one of them fell out. At the time I had two gold fronts, PISSED! The other one was loose too. I went to the dentist and they fixed it up the best they could.

After a few months she got her hostel in King's Cross, but them times Kings cross was serious, so I ended up moving in with her and renting out my place. I wasn't supposed to do that, but it added to my income and I was all about getting that money. Things were looking up and true I wasn't on the ting like that as much, I started to fill back out and look like somebody again. I would only leave her and go missing for 24 hours to smoke, maybe once a month, then come back to her cool. I still wasn't perfect, but I was trying. She was looking after me, she was even learning how to cook so she could cook the food I liked. I wouldn't bring my white stuff around her because she wasn't on it and I wanted to be around her because she was fun to be with. She was good wife material and we were good for a while. She was a little earner too, another thief, not on the level like Kerry, but she would steal garms and take them back, telling them the garms were damaged. Those days, the shops would just give us the cash back. No receipt needed. Things were calm with her for me still, I calmed my hype down as well because I didn't need to keep up with the fuckery with her and she did what she was doing, to make things comfortable for us.

It was Glastonbury time again and after the last time, it was a feature in my calendar. I took like a hundred duds pills, baby powder and wrapped that like it was cocaine along with some bush weed. From I landed in the car park, money me ah mek. Scaled the fence again and it was on same ting. Once I was in, I went back to the front and got my stamp to go and come as I pleased and I started work. I'd been there a few hours making it, then I sold police some duds so they pulled me. I'm thinking, I can't get much for this now because I've got nothing on me, only weed, but they got creative with their charge and charged me with possession with Consent. I'd never heard of such a bullshit charge before in all my life and on top off that, they gave me another 2 years. TWO YEARS ya na. I appealed it and they knocked it down to 15 months.

I told my chick, 'get my rent money from the guy that's living in my yard and give me half.'

She said, 'No problem babes,' and started doing that for me. But after about 6 months I stopped hearing from her and I stopped getting my money, but she was still picking it up from the tenant. I went Bristol Prison first, from summer until it started getting cold. It was 23 hour bang up in that dirty jail. There was nothing nice about that one. I was going through a breakdown, I remember. I couldn't believe I was back in jail. I had to shake myself out of it though, or I wasn't getting through it. That took me about 10 days. I had been refusing to eat and all of that, so I ended up serving the food. I was in Bristol for 4 months before we all had to be moved. It came out that Bristol had asbestos. Everyone got split up into the surrounding area jails. I went to Cardiff. Cardiff was different for real and this shows you how far I was going with this jail ting. No one looked like me and everyone was speaking this Cardiff language them call Welsh. It was alright for me in Cardiff though only because in 4 days I went from normal to an enhanced status. All I had to do was pass a piss test and because I hadn't taken any drugs in a minute I passed, so they put me in a place where it was half decent. I only had to do a month there before they fixed up the asbestos and sent us all back to the Bristol jail, to wait until we were sent out to our next jail, which for me was Dartmoor. This was a weird jail, as we drove towards it I was thinking about all them kids that Brady and Hindley killed. That jail had about 35% black people in it and because we were all so far away from home, we would cling to each other. We should have been applying those same principles on the outside, unity; we all had the same enemy.

The first day I got there they put me in a cell with a broken window. It was freezing and they had me there for about a month, before they moved me over to a better wing. Where I ended up serving food again. Even though that was a half decent job, I still wanted to go home so I was trying to get my appeal as quick as I could. It came up about 5 months into my stay, where they told me one night, pack your things you're going to court in the morning. The next day when I went court for my appeal, the Judge let me walk straight from there. I was so happy! I travelled back to the ends on my own and ended up at my yard in Leytonstone. I was lucky I still had a yard I could go to and the tenant that was still there had to take a room now. I told him simple, 'I'm coming back in here. You're gonna take the front room and I'm taking my bedroom. Just keep paying me my rent and you nice.' So that was it. I'm back on the ends. My chick had violated me and I wanted to take her head off, but I would have gone back to jail if I did. So I holla'd her, just to tell her I'm back on road and not to take any more of my money. She was so surprised I was back, she wanted to link me that same day, but first I asked her,

'have you got my money?'

She stuttered and said, 'no!'

So I told her, 'listen, it's best I don't see you ever.' Me and her done right there, official. I'm out now and I don't want to go back to jail for real, so I'm trying to turn my life around. I went straight to the Job Centre, bright and early the next morning looking a job. I actually got a job, but it was working in a meat factory chopping pig. Imagine I don't even eat pork, but I'm having to chop pig every day because of all the wrong turns I had made in my life. This is what my life had come to now, I'm trying to stay out of trouble. I worked there for 2 months, freezing, cold and wet every day before I said, 'Fuck that!' A full shift was 8 hours, so I fucked that right off and guess what I did? I went back to road, teefing and on top of that in all the time I was in jail, rent arrears had added up. My ex had taken her share and my share of my money and the money the housing was looking was too much, so I couldn't pay it and I lost my yard. I'm sofa surfing all now, as well as still smoking crack with a "ME AGAINST THE WORLD" attitude. I feel vulnerable, but too ful of pride to ask anyone who would help me for help and right now you better believe anyone can get it.

We pick up now at the beginning of my story where I bored up that guy for taking the piss and made a mess in that crack house. Life was getting too much, I was angry with the world and I wasn't taking any more talk. Them guys thinking I'm an average crackhead had to stop. I was a bad man that liked to smoke crack, not a crackhead. That's what I wanted these drug dealers and cats to know now. When I left the yard, I went back to my bredrin's where I had spent the last few weeks sofa surfing, to think about what had happened. I didn't know if anyone had ratted me out, so I wasn't sure if I had new warrants for my arrest. I'd already done 8 years and I didn't want to do any more. But, I was that guy that would cut off my nose to spite my face. I wasn't going to let anyone take the piss and if that meant going back to jail, then that's where I was going. From then I decided, everyone can get it now including them pussy hole drug dealers because the way I saw it, they had taken everything from me, so now I was going to start taking back. Yeah it was time; I guessed they would have called the ambulance and the ambulance would have called the police, so I was bait in that crack house for now. I went to another crack house that them man controlled. This was the day the 3 World Trade Centre buildings came down, building 1, 2 and building 7. I did my surveillance on the yard first, then stopped a crackhead as he came out.

I said, 'Yo who's in the yard?'

The yute said, 'There's some guys in there I don't know, they might be looking for you.' I looked at him then let him go. I wanted to be the one surprising guys. I didn't want any one surprising me. But, I wanted crack, so I said fuck it and knocked the door. My name was ringing on the ends after what I had done. There was a little bit of blatant fear, mixed with shock and anxiety because they didn't know what I wanted. They hoped it was just crack, but it could have been robbery because they knew I was on this ting. This crack house was set in a way where, as you came in, all you had access to was the kitchen and because of what I had done, that's where they were leaving me right now. I was there chilling where cats who came looking food had to wait. If I knew them I would leave them, and they would break me off a ting then bounce. If I didn't know them and they looked at me, I was robbing them, straight. I was on them like flies to shit from I caught eye contact.

'What the fuck you looking at? What you got for me? Peel back your pockets rude boy or I'll bore you up.' That's how I'd give it to them and after I'd taken their tings, I'd give them a few slaps and send them on their way. I did that about 4 times in the hour before one of them screamed out like a little bitch. He actually didn't need to scream like that because I hadn't even slapped him yet, but he was just trying to get the drug dealer's attention. Maybe he thought I cared. I actually really wanted to see what they had to say about me robbing their cats, in their crack house. This one yardie (Merciless) came running to the door to see wha gwan, cutlass in hand ready to try police the yard. I stood there looking in his eye. He looked at me and realised shit, I'm serious. The next ting was, I was talking to this fool in patois. Merciless and the rest of the drug dealers knew me as Yankee. They didn't know my background was Jamaican, so when they saw it was me that shocked them. Apart from the fact I really wasn't in no play play ting with any of them.

I stood there and said, 'You holding cutlass like you gonna do me something with it. Do it, but you better do it good coz if I disarm you, it's not one chop you getting. You getting a bag ah chop.' He saw the realness in my eye and stood down, but I could see he wasn't happy. He just didn't want anything like that with me so he asked me nicely,

'Yankee, please leave the yard.'

I told him, 'put boss man on the phone, I want to talk to him.' The dealer had to call his boss to talk me down and the boss man told the dealer to give me 2 rocks. After that I left casual.

Chapter 10

There was another guy around me called Gotti, who I would hang with sometimes in these crack houses, he was cool. He smoked crack and sold brown, so any time his phone rang it was a £500 shot (sale) he was licking (making). He was kind of maintaining, but saying that, every time he did lick the pipe he would talk about spiders. There were never any spiders on him, but he would say, 'Yo Yanks, get these spiders off me blood.' Drugs had us funny, all in our own way, but other than that he was cool and he paid his drug debts all the time. He felt like because he always paid, he could ask the dealer to tick him some brown (give him some heroin without paying) only for a few hours, so he could make some money. The drug dealer with his ego handled him like all the other junkies, dissing him with a big loud 'NO.' This pissed Gotti off and he knew how I felt about them so he asked me, 'Yo Yanks, come let's rob this place?' But since me and Merciless had our little standoff, we had come to an understanding. At that particular time, I didn't want to because it would have made things sticky for me, remember I'm homeless all now. Even though I couldn't let anybody know it, I actually needed these spots these man were controlling. I was eating from these houses and smoking too, on top of the fact that I could just stay if I wanted to. Don't get it twisted, I didn't like them, trust them, or want to stay but if I didn't have anywhere else to stay, this was a last resort. At the same time though, as I said before I was feeling vulnerable and I didn't like that feeling. Man being able to tell me "No" and I didn't like the place I was in my life, so I was volatile. I said 'No' at the time to man turning over the yard, but the seed had already been planted in my mind, so that "No" could easily turn to a "Yes" at any time.

These times while I was on my face, my Mum and sister were staying at my youngest brother's house. I was tired of sofa surfing from one crack house to the next because even though all these cat knew I was crazy, I still had to worry about guys, friend and foe getting at my pockets while I was sleeping. I really needed somewhere friendly like my brother's house to stay. It was wearing me out, I could feel it, all of these sleepless nights. It just so happened that while I was feeling like this and things were getting desperate for me, I got lucky. My sister was offered a place which she accepted, so her and my Mum were able to move out, making it possible for me to move in with my brother. My little brother couldn't deny me, but he actually made me feel like he didn't want me to stay, like he didn't trust me in his yard or something. I had never done him anything, not even like big brother bullying. *He didn't even give me a key*. I would leave the yard when I wanted to, but would have to stay out until he got back. Sometimes, he wouldn't even listen out for the door bell, so I would have to throw a stone up at the window to make him know I was there. Then he would open the door. Them ways my lickle brother did angle me. On top of the fact that I would give him money and crack spliffs that he would take, but he would still angle me like a stranger. Seeing this from my youngest brother, made me stop and check myself. I wasn't moving right I know. But my brother still shouldn't have been treating me like some random trouble maker. This is how man was treating me on road. It hurt me and true I knew that the police were looking for me, I decided to keep a low profile and try stay away from the crack house Leyton and Leytonstone life.

Trying

In my attempt to get clean, I decided to touch Walthamstow and link Howard. He was Marky's older brother and we had been bredrins from morning. He didn't smoke crack, he just sniffed a little and smoked weed, so I saw myself as cool there. An old school friendly face that was cool, so we were chilling and catching up, then his bredrin turned up. He was a burglar and he talked about all the money he had made on road doing his ting. He actually had a move lined up for the evening, but he needed a whip so we decided to do the move together, true I had my stolen whip outside. He had some things to do before, so he asked me to drop him to his yard first. I did that and told him I'll come back and link him in the appropriate hour, then bounced. I went back to Walthamstow and chilled there until evening, when I headed out back to Stokey to pick him up, to go do this move.

As I'm driving in Hackney, this chick who was riding her bike just fell off in front of the car. I almost run her over, so I stopped to help her up. As I was helping her, I saw she was attractive so we started talking, as I walked her across the road. As we were getting on well, I decided to walk her to her yard, which she said was just around the corner. We walked straight past my new bredrin Joe's hostel and after a quick left and a right, we were there at her yard. She was having trouble opening her front door, so I helped her with that and we went in. I parked off her bike in the passage and followed her to the front room, where we started doing a ting (kissing and feel ups). After a little while she got up and headed to the bedroom. I didn't know where she was going so I asked her and she told me, 'Come and find out.'

I said, 'Cool,' so followed her to her bedroom where we started fucking. This was all normal to me. Fucking gal I just met and this one wasn't gonna be an all-night ting because I already had my agenda and I was still going to do this move. After I beat it, I got up and got myself ready to leave. It was a good beat, so I actually felt bad about fucking and just leaving. So I asked her for her number and she gave it to me.

I told her 'I'll holla you soon,' and headed towards the door, to leave the yard. I didn't know she had a flat mate she lived with, who had heard us. But as I was leaving, I saw her in the passage, she said, 'Hello!'

I said, 'Hello,' back and kept it moving. Now obviously, not recognising me from anywhere she must have went upstairs to her flat mates room to ask who I was. All of that, I didn't stop to think about at the time. I was on my way to go link Joe in the hostel, which I did. He grabbed his things and we rolled out driving from Stokey towards Loughton. Where he had this move planned. It was one arcade, and as we got to Loughton Town Centre we did the move with no long ting. It wasn't what I was expecting, but we took about £500 in coins from the coin machines and split that, then I told him as we were heading back to the ends, come buy a ting for me in this crack house.

He asked me, 'Why don't you want to go in yourself?'

I told him, 'I made a mess in there a little while ago so it's bait for me.' After I told him that, he didn't want to go in either, but he wanted a ting as much as I did so he said, 'Fuck it,' and when we arrived at the spot he went in. After he got the ting, we went back to his spot in Stokey and smoked it til morning, then I left his yard with the intention of going to sort out my Social and maybe even moving into this hostel with him.

A few days later I went back over them sides to link both of them, my bredrin Joe and this new chick. I stopped at the chick's yard first and knocked her door, she looked out the window and I showed myself to her. She gave me a strange look then came to the door. As she opened up she started talking about, 'I think you took advantage of me, you raped me.' I couldn't believe what this chick was talking about. I tried to remind her that she had given me her number and there was nothing about rape that happened that night. But she wasn't having any of it and her same flat mate was right by the door watching what was going on, so it felt like she was putting on a show to her friend. After a while of me trying to convince her and her not having it,

I said 'Ok, I hear what you're saying and if you don't want me to come back to your yard that's fine, I'll never come back.' I left it as that then bounced. After that I kicked right out of Stokey, I didn't link Joe and I didn't hang around. I just kept it moving. Rape ya na! I needed to smoke something for that talk. I went straight to a crack house, I knew I shouldn't really have even been in because it had just been turned over by a next set of youngers, a week or so before. It was bait in there and everyone was on edge. What had happened was, some yutes from the ends had turned up, guns drawn asking for the boss man. They were telling man, 'Open the gate or we gonna start blasting man's heads off.' The boss man had thrown a mattress out the window then jumped to get away. I was standing in the kitchen when it kicked off watching the play. They saw me and said all loud, 'Don't worry Yanks, you're good.' I didn't even recognise these yutes, but when I heard that, I was out. It didn't look good, it could have looked like I had set it up, or at the very least someone was gonna call my name somewhere in this, so I took my bredrin who I was with, Sparks who had just licked the pipe and walked him out and down the stairs. He was so fucked, if I hadn't helped him who knows what would have happened to him. These times the youngers that I had seen in their nappies were these same yutes grown up and wiling out all over East London. I was seeing the ripple effect right here. Crack houses were getting turned over at least 3 times a week, so drug dealers were having to move their spots regular.

Flinni come back into my life around this time on a random one. We knew each other from back in the day, but we were in different crews. I was with the Walthamstow man dem and he was with the Leytonstone man dem. He was a white bree but he was highly respected by the man dem and he had a bag of black gal on him. Flinni was on both, white and brown and he was on the gear hard, but true he was a don from back in the day and still maintaining, he was respected. We had done a little bird in Pentonville together and we had talked about when we touch road, how we were going to do this ting together. I had got out before him and forgot about that jail house talk because out of sight was out of mind in my world. But when we linked up on a random one, it was like it was supposed to be. I would have even said it was perfect timing, me in one crack house and him just getting out of jail and finding his way to the same crack house. Me and Gotti were sitting down getting high when Flinni turns up. It was almost that same day we started robbing Off Licenses.

At 2am every night, we would drive this stolen whip, fully loaded with all the tools we needed to break into shit and steal, til we found an Off License to break into. We would break the lock, lift up the shutter, smash the window, run in there and steal all the things that would make us quick money. It was a good and consistent eat, so I was buying my crack no problem and the cats that I would usually eat, were getting left alone a little now. The drug dealers were seeing me consistently buying and not causing the other cats any problem, so they dropped their guard a little with me. You could even say; our relationship got a little better. Not that it was good or anything, but I went to link one of my long time fellow smokers and got to find out that his yard was where they were packaging, before they would send the food out to the trap houses. It seemed like they didn't mind me seeing or knowing that and being around, while they were doing their ting. They were out here acting like I was nice, even. On top of that, they had the nerve to ask me to watch their gear (drug), *them gone too far.*

Obviously I said, 'Cool,' and as soon as they left, so did I with all their drugs. Me, Gotti and Flinni had a party that night, straight. A bag of girl in a next crack house. One of the dealers I robbed even turned up at the party, we were having. We had these girls standing up on stools dancing, putting on strip teases, all for the love of the crack. I wasn't really watching it at the time but they were hating us. All of them from the crack whores to the drug dealers that I had robbed. It was a twisted way of thinking; the crack whores would only respect you if you treated them like shit. We were out here giving away the crack and they were out here trying to work brain on us. But the drug dealers who would slap them about and treat them like shit, they would respect highly and not try anything with. Now the drug dealers knew I had robbed them. I had to watch it even though they weren't saying anything. They could have paid someone to try do me something if they didn't want to do it themselves, or something else that I wasn't thinking about, but I should have been. That move right there set off a chain of events.

After we had that party, I linked the guy whose yard I had robbed like nothing had happened. I even told him I was selling because I still had nuff left on me. I couldn't use all of it that one night, so it made sense I put out the word. After I left there, I went to another crack house where I went into the kitchen to bill it and sell to them too. But in this yard the vibe was a little different. I could hear people upstairs talking about me. Talking about the moves I was on and the money I was making, then I saw these 2 bree's from Forest Gate come in the yard. I'd seen them a few times before, but I didn't know them like that. When one of them started coughing hard, I clocked the play instantly. This guy was big and I could tell he was on it. The next guy was a slim light skinned bree and even though I knew they came together, the light skinned one decided he's going to stand on the other side of the kitchen. It was a blatant distraction ting. I was just about to lick the pipe as well, but when I saw that, I decided to build a crack spliff instead. I knew these man didn't lick the pipe and for me who licks the pipe, a spliff was a calm ting. But, for a man who didn't lick the pipe, the spliff was like the pipe would be for me. I offered them a crack spliff, knowing that they would feel like I would have, if I had licked the pipe. They took that and built 2 spliffs, as I stood up and watched them. As they lit and smoked that, I knew I had them now how they would have had me, but I stayed cool.

I started talking to them, 'Look, I done see the play and I know the play. I've been doing what you've come to try with me from long time, but it doesn't make sense you come war with me. It makes sense we do this ting together. Look, you haven't had to do me nothing to get a ting. The guys who sent you ain't looked after you like I'm looking after you now have they?' That made them think about what I was saying. They could see I was serious and by now they were high. This one was sticky, so as I had them in that deep thought, I acted like my phone was vibrating. I answered it talking to myself and acting like someone was outside waiting for a ting. I told man I'm coming as I walked out the kitchen, down the passage and out the door, down the stairs and into my whip to roll out. I wondered who set that up, I had my suspicions. I think it was one chick I knew, but I allowed that one because I saw that as my karma.

I was living reckless anyway, so I didn't care, it was all about the money and I was a serious opportunist. Every day I left my yard something would happen. Those 2am Off License eats were a nice side hustle, but nothing was exempt. Day time I had to eat too and I was now staying in Walthamstow feeling like I needed to lick a big ting. All this running up and down for hundreds was long. I made sure I kept my ear to the ground, so when I heard something big was happening with some guys from my block and guys from off the ends. This was the one I had been waiting for. I knew it was just big money these man did deal with, so I decided to look about eating that. I didn't mind war and that's if the out of towners found me. So I got all the information I needed for when it was next happening and decided I was gonna do this move with Gotti. On the day, we positioned ourselves perfect, so when we saw the guy with the money get out his car, I put the machine in his face and he didn't resist. It was a quick ting and Gotti grabbed the briefcase and we walked out of view, then we ran to the car and drove off down the road to Queens Road, where we checked this woman who smoked on a sly. She didn't bait up herself or her yard, so we could go there and chill. When we got there, we opened the briefcase and there was a quick 20 bags in there for me and Gotti to split. I was expecting a little more, but 10 bags each was a nice day's work. After we split it Gotti bounced and I went and bought another whip. I was crumbling inside, but I wouldn't let anyone see that. I would buy things that would keep people assuming that I was ok and maintaining, but I wasn't and this made me vicious, it was my self defence mechanism. After I bought the whip, I rolled over to my local crack house to show off. I knew guys in there were hating and they didn't want to see me shine, so I was trying to put all that shine in their face. I pulled up and they embraced me with the bullshit, acting like they were happy for me and shit, then one of them mentioned he had some girls in Chingford that we could check,

'Smokers like us,' he said.

I was on it, so we started driving my new whip down towards Chingford to link these crackheads. It was me, the bree that I had robbed his yard of the drug dealer's food and one next bree. It was a sunny day, but it was cold. It was November 2001 and I'd been up for 10 days straight. Any time I felt I was dozing off, I would lick the pipe again. It was the paranoia. I couldn't trust anyone and the crack had everyone in their own madness. As I said before, even though people knew if I caught them trying to get at my pockets I would look blood, they would still try, so I was just trying to stay up forever when I was around them.

We were driving down Highams Park all now and the heating's on because it's cold, but I was so tired I started dozing off behind the wheel. I guess it was the heat as well as everything else. Next thing I know everything went black, then I heard loud banging and I woke up with my nose bloodied and smashed in on the steering wheel. Everybody froze for a few second's but when my head cleared, the first thought was keep it moving. As we were getting out the car, the guy I was with went into the glove compartment and took out the book with the information about the car in it. I wondered why at the time, but I was just trying to get out of there so I didn't bother ask. I had crashed into about 5 parked cars. With all the noise, people came out their houses to ask if we were alright. But we ignored them as we walked down the road. Obviously, we fucked off going to link the girls. As we buss the corner we bounced. When we got to a safe distance and we began walking I told man, 'Don't say nothing about what just happened, when we get back to the ends.'

He said, 'Don't worry, I won't say nothing.' I didn't want them guys in the house to know what had happened, there was a bag of them man that I knew would love to hear that. I was really trying to hold that one down. On top of the fact that I had just bought the shit, so as we got back to the yard, we went into separate rooms. The pussy started talking the ting straight away, but whispering so I wouldn't hear him. I knew he was talking my business though because I could hear people responding to him and giggling. *This pussy talking my business already*! I got mad as I went into the room and rass him with 2 licks straight. He did stand up and take them licks. No one said anything, then I left it. I hoped he would have got the message, with them rass lick I did give him. I came back a few days later to smoke again and this time now, I'm in the bedroom building a ting. I know it's his yard and all that, but my business is my fucking business and I done already told him to not say anything. He already got 2 clap, but he still wants to talk my business, laughing about what had happened, like the licks I gave him were a joke. I moved to him again in his yard, but this time with my borer. I was so mad but I decided not to bore him because I would have murdered him in there, so I just rassed him in his head with the handle until I heard him squeak a bag of squeaks, like a captured mouse. I had to fuck him off coz I was feeling like I might really do him something serious, if he kept taking the piss. There were plenty crack houses around for me to get my ting to smoke, so I stopped linking him.

Me and Flinni had done our usual night time move, but we hadn't eaten so well that night, so we decided to hit the road during the day, to try a ting. One of Flinni's guys owed him some money, so the guy dropped a little whip on him. I had just crashed my whip, so Flinni's was good to go with. We left out from Leyton in this whip and headed towards West End, to see what we could eat. I liked West End because it was full of crooks trying to either rob the tourists or even each other, so we just fitted in nice to that boiling pot of fuckery. We parked up on a side road and got out to see what was popping, but for some reason as soon as we started walking, we both felt like the heat was on us. It didn't take long before we decided to get back in the whip and bounce. We jumped in ready to roll out, but almost instantly the boy dem was on us. I was driving and this car was little with no power. We weren't going to get away if I didn't do some mad driving and ended up going through some bollards that the police couldn't fit through so we lost them.

As we were in West End already, we decided to go link one of Flinni's girls over Battersea. Since we were driving in that direction. Reckless behaviour carried on all the way to South, with me driving down a one-way road the wrong way. I had to reverse onto a roundabout. If the police had seen what we were keeping up with, they would have been on us, but no one saw, so we kept it moving and about 15 minutes later, we were at her yard. This chick was a smoker, but her yard wasn't a trap house. When we arrived she told us she didn't have any crack so we needed to go get some. The trap house was only a block away. I gave them my money and waited on the staircase of one tower block as they went to get it. I knew about them ends, so I respected it and held my corner. A few minutes later they came back and gave me the ting, but it was small and that's where our problems started. I didn't say it was small straight away, but it was. *Was Flinni taking the piss?* I decided to hold it down til we got back to the yard. But as soon as we got back and I blammed (hit) the ting, I got dark on them. I started pacing around. We were going to smoke the ting together, but after they showed me their face I decided I'm not sharing my ting with them and I wanted someone to say something. As I've said before, I always liked to do man something, in the name of self-defence. This guy, supposed to be my boy, Flinni had bumped me so he deserved the clap down, but I was going to feel even better if he made the move on me first. He knew I wasn't playing though so he didn't say anything. He was a man where if he thought he was going to get something out of bumping someone, he would play along and this is what was going on here. His girl had done the move and he had stood by and watched. I put it on her in front of him, I made her know the ting was small, so I'm smoking all of it on my own and don't take man for a dickhead. I had already made my mind up that if anyone violated, everyone was getting it. After I smoked my ting we left, heading back to the ends. I carried on the darkness to Flinni when we got back by taking the car. He didn't say a thing and we kept it moving.

Day in, day out more bullshit, hanging around crack houses and bleaching (staying up all night). Hanging around people I didn't like, all because I didn't want the good people in my life to see what my life had become. It was a blur and my long time bredrin Yanky Wayne had been with me for a few days. We had been floating from crack house to crack house getting high, til

Wayne ask me to drop him home. Even though I was fucked and I shouldn't have been driving, I saw Wayne as a bredrin so I did that for him. I got him back to his yard safe ready to sleep, then I bounced acting like I had somewhere else to go. Really I was just heading back to the crack house. It was rush hour early morning, everyone going to work and I wasn't on the long ting, so I was driving erratic. I took over a few cars on a mad other side of the road ting, then tried to cut back in, but the brakes failed me and I crashed into this space cruiser. That space cruiser got banged so hard, it crashed into the car in front of it. It was fucked, I had no time to be dazed, it's almost like I was getting used to crashes, so I jumped out and walked off down the road. The way it was busy and the way it happened, people were definitely expecting me to run, but people had to watch me a little different when I casually walked off. When I buss that corner though, I kept it moving. I buss bare corners til I ended up back at Wayne's yard, banging on his door. Imagine, I'd just dropped him off there, but now he's not answering. I'm banging in desperation but nothing, so I had to leave the yard and walk on back streets, all the way back to Leyton. I headed straight back to the crack house and it was the same ting again, it was like a trigger, bad things happened and I smoked more crack to ease the pain.

Losing Loved Ones

Chapter 11

It was a very stressful time and maybe it was showing, along with all the whispers on road about what I'd been keeping up with because it got to the stage where, I would turn up at a crack house and they would look through the peep hole, see it was me and not let me in.

I would hear man saying, 'It's Yanks outside you know. I beg you don't let him in.' I was fucking homeless as well, but I couldn't let any of them feel like I needed them or cared. The drug dealers would let me in because it was all about the money to them and now I was just trying to be calm. I realised I was just baiting up myself and if I kept making a mess at these yards, it would just be another yard I couldn't chill in, so I started holding it down. I even decided to put a little business to Merciless, true I didn't fuck with the brown. I told him 'I'll buy some brown and you sell it and we go the 50/50 on the profit.' He was on it, so I started off with a quarter. He was selling crack for another guy and selling the brown for me. It was working and money started coming in. True that was going well,

Merciless told me, 'I want you to take my cousin out with you when you get any big jobs come up.' These guys respected me, even though I was a smoker and that made me feel a bit better about the shit life I was living. I was homeless and I didn't want society to see me like this, let alone my family or friends. But for my drug dealer peers to ask me this, made me feel like I'm still something, as fucked up as it was them asking me that. I thought about it and told him, 'I'll get back to you on that,' I wasn't sure I wanted Merciless' cousin rolling with me like that, we weren't that cool.

One evening as I was looking for a move. I linked back up with a long time rasta bredrin called Sinclair. We smoked together before and he was still on it. Now he had a different link where we could get 8ths for a lot cheaper. I had been paying almost double, so I gave him the P's (money) and he came back with the 8th. The ting was decent too, so now I've got Merciless selling the brown for me and I've got crack to sell again. I was moving in my mind and this worked, for a few days. I would touch all the local crack houses, sit down selling the ting and smoke it.

The night my lifestyle came to haunt me was finally here. I'm in a crack house and the guy I bored up in that other crack house came in the yard bredin (trying to be nice) me like we were friends. I was trying to be calm and leave the fuckery, so I was being civil when he asked me, 'Yo Yanks, you want to buy this gun from me.' I was surprised he wasn't trying to stick me up with it to be honest. It was an old time, come like pirate's gun. I took it and gave it a little once over. It wasn't something I could of work with really, it was too old so I told him 'Nah,' I don't want it. If I had liked it, the old me might have taken it.

He said 'Cool,' then bounced. I didn't think anything of it, as I built another spliff. Then it all got serious about 20 minutes later. I'm in the kitchen and I hear BANG, BANG, BANG. The police had their battering ram working. It was about 4 in the morning and I was just getting ready to lick the pipe again. 'FREEZE, DON'T MOVE, GET DOWN ON YOUR FUCKING BELLIES NOW, ALL OF YOU CUNTS. DONT FUCKING MOVE,' It felt like they were telling me to stop breathing, it was like that and it felt like a set up. *Imagine I had bought that gun*. Big machines up close in my face. Machine guns pressed against the back of my head. I was nervous and they had the yard under control. The dealer in the yard instantly called out my name, like I'm the big man in the yard. That pissed me off especially because out of all these drug dealers I'd dealt with over the years, this one had shown me a face I could reason with. So much so I would buy my rocks from him and even buy him a Guinness. Now he's talking about I'm the guy. I had my pipe in hand ready to lick it. *I was always balling user* and I intended to play up to that fact, but with this guy talking that shit, I could see it might get a little sticky.

They gathered us up and took us to Leyton Police Station, where they gave us single cells. They had me there all night questioning me about my part in that crack house, bring up that robbery from back in the day Brixton with The General. Trying to do me on a conspiracy to supply but the evidence wasn't strong enough. So I thought they were going to give me bail. I knew they didn't want to do that, but what could they do if the evidence wasn't there. As I sat there quite happy with the thought I was getting out, they came back to me and said, 'where not giving you bail because you have a warrant on a rape charge with Stokey Police.'

I was like, 'What? I don't know what you on about,' but then I remembered that chick had said she felt like I had taken advantage of her, even raped her she said. It all started to make sense and no bail meant back to jail. Long!

They put me in Pentonville for a week first, then they sent me up to Belmarsh to spend Christmas. True Belmarsh is a max security jail, it was dead. 23 hour bang up meant that not much of anything other than you and your cell mate was going on. Lunch and exercise, was it. After Belmarsh they sent me to Brixton. Brixton was alright, it was the best part of my time on remand, up until my court case. I went to the Old Bailey first and I'm thinking fucking hell, they are trying to send me down for long. It was a quick one in and out, where it seemed like they just wanted to see me and get my name in the system. No bail obviously, remanded back to Brixton. I couldn't talk to anyone about my charge except my solicitor. No one in there knew I was in on a rape charge and because I was at my lowest point, before I went jail, I hadn't been talking to my family. I definitely wasn't going to be reaching out to them now I was in this situation, so I suffered this one in silence. The next date for Court was just before they were going to wrap up for Christmas. They moved the trial from the Old Bailey to Southwark and when they did that, I thought that was a good thing. I thought they had downgraded the seriousness of my case. But, all of this was just preliminaries. They would ask me one or two questions then send me back to the cells, until the meat wagon came to take me back to jail. This happened for a few months until March 2002, when my trial began. It was me and my Solicitor against the world I thought, until my solicitor started talking a bag of shit.

He said, 'If you go guilty, you are going to get less, but if you get found guilty you going to get a life sentence.' *I was thinking, I've never heard this bullshit before and how can I plead guilty when I ain't done it.*

I told him, 'Nah I'm not pleading guilty to this, I don't care.' So, we are in court now and I'm realising that they are all in it together and this pussy solicitor I'm thinking is here to fight my case ain't here fighting for me. *He even acted disappointed that he hadn't convinced me to go guilty, like he was going to get a bonus if I had.* It started off with them giving their evidence. When it was my turn to talk, due to the fact I felt all alone, I didn't want to go into the dock to be cross-examined. I just told them to listen to my police interview because I was sticking to what I had said there. So they listened and they definitely heard my passion. I was explaining exactly what happened and because I really hadn't done it, I was talking just like that. But, racism was playing a part in this. If I had thought about it, to a white chick that's just come out her bedroom and seen me, "a black dude" she has never seen before, passing her in her corridor, then she goes upstairs and the chick I've been fucking acts like she doesn't know what her flatmate is talking about. Then I turn up 2 days later and put a face to the person the flat mate was talking about. She doesn't want to look loose, I understand, but this was a big charge and now she's said it, she has to stick to it. Then to go to a corrupt and racist Police Force and say that I had raped her, after everything I had done. All the cards were stacked against me for real. On top of that, she stands up and gives them evidence, then her flat mate, then the police. I was a prolific criminal, so it wasn't looking good. But, then the Doctor came and gave evidence in my defence.

He said, 'There isn't any bruising and I couldn't find anything that suggested rape,' on top of the fact that she had given me her number, I still felt I could fight this case. But when it was all said and done, my evidence in their racist eyes wasn't good enough. I was convicted of it. They gave me a life sentence on a 6-year tariff and I just couldn't believe it. *They had just brought out a new law, about 3 years before called 2 strikes, then they called it IPP.* This was a sentence where you just didn't know when you were getting out. Of all the crimes I had committed, they gave me 6 years for rape. It was a massive head fuck, especially because I hadn't raped anyone and now they were sending me to Wormwood Scrubs. The wing they put me on in Scrubs was half mains and half sex offenders. The mains were guys that either had long criminal careers, or their crimes were serious, either Class A drug dealers, armed robbers or murderers. *My criminal career had been extensive, this is why they sent me to Scrubs.*

I was only there 2 days when this tall skinny yute got shipped in. He was young, but he looked like man could get a name off his back if they done him something because he was tall. On the first day when man was serving food, the jail man dem asked him, 'What you in for?' I'm not sure if he told them, or they already knew, but he got his teet lick out for being a rapist. True he was young and scared, he gave the aura like he really is, so they dealt with him accordingly. No one asked me why I was in and because of how I carried myself, I was in with the main crew from I landed. I went to the main guy running the wing for weed and before I knew it, I was rolling with him. Smoking together and doing tings. After that, Scrubs came like road because of how much everything I needed was there for me. Weed on tap, drink on tap and even hard Jamaican food on tap. I was on the Lifers Wing and the screws couldn't really fuck with a lifer. What were you really telling a man who was going to spend the rest of his life in jail. It was here where I started seeing the guys with the 25-year recommendation, wrapped around their sentence. Looking at my sentence after looking at theirs I thought *ok*, maybe I can get out then.

Right there I deciding to fix up, even though it was hard on that wing because everything was there. I didn't even hold a phone myself, but I had guys giving me phones to call my people on the outside whenever I liked. It was difficult, but I tried not to get sent to the block. *The 18 months I did in Scrubs was alright.*

Then they told me to pack my tings because I was getting shipped out to the Isle of Wight the next day. The reason why was because I was with the man dem on the wing and we were all faces. It wasn't that I was hiding it because I really wasn't guilty, but I didn't want anyone to see me go through that door. Where they did this Sex Offenders Course. They were telling me that I needed to do it before I was going to be eligible for parole. I would have preferred to do all or most of my bird in The Scrubs, then get shipped out towards the end to do that course, but they just shipped me out. *They weren't making things comfortable for me.*

Isle of Wight was supposed to be a jail where you stayed for between 3 and 5 years, but they kicked me out of there after about 5 months because I was just making a mess. This jail was full of sex offenders and on top of that, there were no drugs. It was like a rehab jail with a bag of nonces (Sex Offenders) I wasn't ready for the rehab and I definitely didn't want to be around these nonces. They didn't even have a tv for me and they were making me wait weeks. It reached a point where I had to have a meeting with the Prison Officer, one rank below the Governor.

He's asked me, 'What seems to be the problem?' So, I told him and made a joke like, 'Is it because I'm black?' It must have been because I didn't see how the guy could get vex with me for complaining about my living conditions and terminate the interview. From there, they were trying to tell me that I couldn't even have a tv. *They got man on 23 hour bang up and they expect me to ride it without even a tv.* I kicked off for that obviously, so they sent me to the block. They held me there for 3 weeks, then sent me to another wing where I finally got a tv. That was something, but because in their mind I was trouble, they fucked with me for the course. I was brought here supposedly to do this course, but after the Governor asked the Psychologist if she thinks I'm ready and the Psychologist talked to me briefly, she told the Governor, she dosen't think I'm ready to do the course yet and I should wait a little while. From I heard that, I wasn't trying to be cool. Then they fucked with my employment, which meant I only had unemployment money, £2.50 a week. *What the fuck was that even in the prison world*. I had to make private money as a barber to have my little basics. If I wasn't a barber, I would have been with the lowest wage man in the jail.

Life went on like this for a few weeks with the ups and downs of jail, then one day I decided to phone home and see what was happening, on the ends. I phoned my bredrin little David and he asked me if I had heard what had happened to Kerry. I hadn't, then he broke the news that she had died of a drug overdose, *fucking hell*! I wondered wha gwan for our daughter and I was where I was. I couldn't reach out to her now, even to find out anything or even ask her how she was feeling. My mental state was a madness and my relationship with my daughter, what could I say, I didn't even have one, so I wasn't good to be talking to her about her Mum at that time. It hit me hard, but I couldn't dwell on it because I was going through a lot in the shit called Isle of Wight. Still trying to get off that fucking island! More of the same shit day in day out, surviving off man dem looking out for me and my anger.

They were restricting everything, even my smoke. I was mad with all of them Screw pussy holes, so they were trying to keep me on the block, then I got my next bad news. My brother's then girlfriend turned wife hunted me down, none of my family did. She found me to tell me my Grandad had passed. I think he had Alzheimer's in the end and that's what killed him. That one hit me hard too. He was my bredrin. A big man for me, but when I was around he would treat me on a level. One of those mischievous type of old man and in that moment *I remembered his laugh*. It sounded like he was dying as he got older, so my Mum would tell us not to make him laugh. *When I heard that I was numb*. I was missing important things in my life and it was taking its toll on me. I had to act normal, but there wasn't anything normal about this life I was living. I had thought jail was a bad boy ting and I was earning my stripes doing these sentences, but now I was seeing the reality of jail and the system. It had us happy to work as slaves just to get out of 23 hour bang up, year in, year out. To think that this life was cool was ridiculous, man laying down with man and they was telling me, I can't get out until I do this course. It was all bullshit and on top of that, before I was even eligible to do the course, I had to admit to doing the crime. I obviously had a problem with that because I really hadn't done it, but it was either I never admit and stay in jail for ever, or I admit, and they let me do the course, giving me a possibility of one day getting out. I was wasting away in there, while everyone else was doing something to progress. So after much soul searching, I decided to admit to this crime I had not committed, for the opportunity to get out one day. I was struggling, because this bang up was rough. The only time I was with everyone else was at exercise and association. I didn't think I was going to make it through this one.

They came to me one day on more bullshit telling me to come with them to do a piss test.

I told them 'wait til I've finished eating my food.'

They told me, 'Nah come now,' but I didn't. I went to my cell and ate my food, so they locked me in. 2 hours later they unlocked me and told me to stop by the Governor's on my way to the block. I stopped off to hear this fool talking about, 'there has been 3 reports of you bullying other inmates.' That was a lie; I hadn't bullied any of the inmates. It was the screws that had made up the accusations, so I said, 'Fair enough,' and continued on down to the block, not knowing how serious they were making this ting for me. From then they wanted me out, but it wasn't that easy to get someone out when they were on the block. Other jails would want to know why you were on the block because they didn't want trouble coming to their jail, so it was kind of difficult to get the transfer. It was either that or you would get sent from block to block, where the prisons would swap block prisoner for block prisoner. The only way you would get on a wing if you were coming from the block, was if the new block you were going to was full. If that was the case, you would get locked up in your cell on the wing, where other inmates could open your cell and ask you questions. If you lied about anything they asked, you were in trouble. *Prison justice*!

I'd had enough of this block shit and this just topped it off. Guys on the block were supposed to get their canteen first, but when it came to me, they were telling me there wasn't any record of my canteen. I said, 'Oh that's convenient.' Obviously thinking they had either given it to one of their rat boys, or they had taken my burn and smoked it themselves.

I'm saying to them, 'Look, if you can't find my canteen, let me get a burn from one of the cleaners or someone.' The boss of the block opened my door with his two other screws and told me to my face, 'Fuck off,' then grabbed me in one cage fighting move and tried to put me to the floor. I grabbed him straight, picked him up and carried him into my room. I gripped him and didn't let go, his two boys were there trying to get me off him, but it wasn't working. One of them tried to break my finger trying to get me off, but not even that worked. I had this fucker and he was not going anywhere. When they saw that, one of the Screws came out the cell and pressed the emergency buzzer. A bag of Screws came running. When the rest of the Screws got there, they overpowered me and lifted me up, legs dangling and carried me to the strip cell where they cut my clothes off my skin and left me naked in that cold cell, end of December times.

For not taking the piss test and defending myself like that the Governor gave me 14 days on the block. I wanted to be with the man dem because it was Christmas so I was pissed about that, but I thought cool, fuck it. After 13 days I'm thinking right I'm off the block tomorrow. Then the head of security governor came and said that there had been 13 more allegations against me of bullying on the wing!

He said, 'we're going to keep you on the block for Good Order And Discipline (GOAD), whilst we wait for a van to pick you up and take you to Full Sutton, top security A Cat jail. I'm a B Cat Prisoner so I wasn't even supposed to be in an A Cat prison, but I preferred to be in them real prisons because the man dem in those jails are real. You know where you stand with them man.

The journey to get there took 2 days. They had me sleeping in other jails along the way with all the processes, like I'm staying there. It was so long.

I finally got to Full Sutton and the Screws are telling me they are putting me on the numbers wing. That's where you go when you're a fucking wrongen, either informer or rapists end up on this wing. So I'm telling them, 'Nah, I want to go on the mains.'

The Screws were telling me 'You can't be on the mains for your own safety.'

I'm telling them 'The mains is my comfort zone,' but they weren't having it and put me on the Numbers Wing. *I had to start sizing man up*. Full Sutton was up North, so you had Manchester man, Leeds man, Birmingham man and Sheffield man all together. Me as a London man had to latch on to other London man because them up North man were serious on their gang ting.

Full Sutton was a jail where you could build up yourself though. I started with the gym seriously and eating properly. It wasn't easy to get drugs there because it was top security. All man could smoke was tobacco. We weren't having late nights, going out to party or anything like that, so I used it as training. The only sad thing was, I was finding this discipline hard in jail. It was a jail where a lot of freaky shit was going on. Man would talk about they are not gay, but they got next man sucking their dick. I saw man sell their backside for £5. I would catch certain man doing transactions with batty man, after they swear say them bun fire pon batty man. They had me on wing with man who had been caught fucking animals. Even man like Dennis Nilsen the serial killer, I was sharing this wing with. *This prison was serious even on the Numbers Wing.* After about a week, they gave me a job in a sewing workshop. I was making clothes for the whole prison system and going to education learning English and Maths level 1 and 2 and Computers, just to familiarise myself with them for when I got out.

Time To Reflect

Chapter 12

In this jail now, I started to see how long jail really was. There were guys in there that I looked at and really did not want to ever be like. Some man had been on the same wing for 12 years, cleaning the same landing. Real no hopers who actually didn't want their date of release to come. *I didn't want to ever feel like that about jail*. Some guys would get released and do a crime to get brought back and for all the time I'd done in jail, I couldn't see how a man could ever feel like jail was alright enough to try to come back. I didn't want this any more, so I got my head down and started going library and gym. Eating reasonably well, to the point where I even started to enjoy cooking. *And this is when I started to grow mentally as well as physically*. I began to see life from a different perspective. After being in jail for 3 years, half of my 6 year sentence, they finally put me on that Sex Offenders Course I needed to get on, before I had any chance of getting out.

They put me in a class with 9 man and this course was basically each of us one after the other telling the rest of the group our life story. It was like they wanted to break you down, to then build you back up. It was a 6 month course and in the beginning looking at these faces I didn't like any of them. These guys were seeing me at my most vulnerable, so it was difficult in the beginning being the prideful man that I am. But, as time went on and I heard other people's stories, there were parts of some of their stories that I related to. We would come to a understanding on that, like the abuse or the drugs or the violence, that might have been shared experiences as youth growing up. But the freaks, I couldn't ever agree with and I couldn't do them anything. *I had to act like I was cool with some of the depraved things they had done.* It was mad really because with all the time I had already done, no jail had me wanting to touch road like this jail. *It was a real sentence jail.* Everyone was on big birds and you would be lucky if you saw one man get released in the entire year. Sometimes a man wouldn't get released in 2 years. With that jail, I didn't even think about my family or friends coming to visit me, it was to far. Also because it was top security, visitors would have to go through madness and bare different searches on top of dogs, before you finally got to see man. I accepted the fact that I had to do my time on my own in this one and that made me want to get out even more. *Fuck a bad boy ting, jail was long.* The whole life I had lived up until this point was long. I had nothing to show for all this time I was spending in a cage except for missing the very important milestones in my life.

It was six years of this I had to do before they were going to consider me for release. I didn't actually realise what that really meant was after six years, my sentence was just starting. IPP stood for Imprisoned for Public Protection, so they were going to monitor me until they felt like I was no longer a threat to the public. I'd finally reached a place in my life where I saw that I could actually get old and die in jail. That's when they started to play games with me. I went on certain pre-parole board meetings after I completed my first course and because the Psychologist felt like; for whatever reason I needed to do the course again and I disagreed, I was considered non-compliant. This meant I couldn't get privileges, like extra money or canteen. No extra gym, sometimes I even got deducted on the phone and my visits. *Everything could be deducted until you ended up with nothing.* They were trying to press my buttons, but I could see what they were doing, so for that reason. I wasn't going to have a moment and freak out even though at times it was hard.

I knew I needed to stay focused to progress and after a few

months I got a transfer to this therapeutic jail, all the way in Derby. In this jail you had a main and a therapeutic community. It was actually half decent to look at with regards to the facility. *Each guy had their own cell and shower*. In this prison the Governor wasn't called the Governor, he was the Director. This jail didn't have wings, it had communities, so we didn't have wing meetings, we had community meetings and if you didn't want to go play bingo on the weekend, you were considered anti-social. Inmates would talk shit looking to impress the Screws talking about, 'You know you should participate in our bingo nights and it's good to be social,' knowing that the Screws were watching and would put that down on their file, that they understood socialising. In the community meetings the inmates would take positions such as Chairman and Vice Chair. Madness, that kind of bullshit. Sometimes a fool would call for a group meeting when you were on your association. If you decided you didn't want to go for the group meeting, your name would be mentioned the next day with bad connotations attached. Fights would break out because of that. You would have man when they tried to call man out, switch and remind them that, 'don't think because we're in this therapeutic jail that I won't fix you. You know if we were on the mains, you wouldn't be going on like that.' Man would get moved too, real quick.

This jail was the type of jail where 90% of the people in there didn't mind being a rat. Only 10% of us played by the rules and for this reason, I really didn't like this jail where everyone was acting. They would act like they weren't doing shit and sell you all the way down the river. For instance, if your eye was red, they wouldn't say anything to just you. They would wait until this big community meeting then try and expose you, knowing that they had protection around them. If you moved to a man who ratted you out in therapy, then things would get bad for you quickly. This Jail was basically an experiment, and we were the guinea pigs. On top of that, the way they saw it in the system was, if you couldn't maintain your composure in there, then there would be no forward progression for you. Furthermore, if you went in front of the parole board and that was on your record, they were always refusing your release.

Get Me Out Of Here

After about 10 months I couldn't take any more of this Therapeutic bullshit, so I told them I wanted to leave and I had to put in a notice, telling them all of my reasons. I just couldn't take kissing ass in there anymore, especially because I couldn't see any forward movement. It took them 2 months to get a van to pick me up and take me out of there. I was trying to get a jail back on the ends, or as close to the ends as possible. I was tired of this country ting, like I'm a country man all now. I'm trying to move forward but because I was asking to leave this therapeutic jail before my 18 months was up, I knew they probably wouldn't let me move forward, so I was saying at least let me move to the side then. Keep me in a jail like this, but put me on the mains or something. But I was being blocked. I would put in applications for a decent transfer and the screws would either lose the paperwork, or tell me they didn't have any space in that jail. My Solicitor told me that part of my clause going to this jail was, if I dropped out before my 18 months, I would have to go back to the jail I came from, or go to a jail even worse. My argument was, I hadn't been kicked out or been sent to the block for anything. I just didn't want to be in that jail any more. They were not having it though and they used a bag of delays and stalling tactics to keep me wasting time, until they finally got their act together and sent a van to pick me up and shipped me out, but back to Full Sutton.

As soon as I heard I was going back to Full Sutton, I wanted to at least go back to the same way that I had it when I left. I wanted the same wing with the same man dem and all that, but when I got back, all the man dem had been separated and they put me on a totally different wing. I had to wait until work or education to link up the man dem. From there I started to meet the new man on the wing and some of them that had heard of me.

It took me a few months, but it got back to the way it was before I left it on this new Full Sutton wing. The politics was, the 10 months I had done in therapy they made it not count for anything. The top Screw told me, I still needed to do the same course again, but I was refusing. I knew that refusing that course would make things harder for me, but I didn't care. It was the fact that the course was basic and I knew I had passed it already. I had passed it before I started it, but it was a game they were playing with my life. *I still didn't fully understand yet.*

I kept getting onto the Governor about my transfer. In my face, he would act cool, but behind my back he was blocking me, refusing to help me progress. By now I had my Solicitor involved, so before it started looking like he was doing something wrong, or on purpose, he finally got the van to come for me and I got shipped out. With this on my report though, they were making it seem like I was not doing anything to reduce the risk to the public, like these bullshit courses proved anything.

I've Got No Choice

I'd been in the prison system this time now over my 6 years tariff. I was due to see the parole board, but they postponed it because the Screw had finally decided to get me moved to Kingston in Portsmouth, which was another lifer's jail. *They were taking the piss.* Why would they decide to move me when my parole hearing was coming up, like my main objective wasn't to get out? Imagine I was supposed to be out long time, but the parole board sent me a letter telling me, I now have to wait another 2 years before I would be able to see them again. *2 years ya na*! I accepted this was my punishment and I deserved punishing for some of the things I had done, but I had my reasons and this was the problem with this racist system. *They didn't give a shit about black people's reasons, so many of which they had actually caused.* They had me up and down in this prison system like my name was yo-yo. I was way up North one minute and now they were moving me way down South. At least man dem round here were sounding more like London man.

In there, we had more freedom than Full Sutton, but it was still prison. Everyone in there was on a gym ting. We had gym 3 times a day. I got there June 2008 with a plan. I just wanted to get my C Cat and move off to a better jail. That was a progressive move. I started going on one drugs course. It wasn't really a course, but there was a woman who wanted to talk to me about my drug use. So I engaged her as part of my sentence plan, along with trying to stay out of trouble, to be proactive and focused on what I needed to do to get out at the earliest possible time. I took a job in there, in their workshop. They had me there for 2 months, then after that I put in the application to work in the laundry. This job had privileges; you could charge extra P to private wash man's clothes, so I was kind of alright in this jail. I could order from the catalogue and the food was nicer. I could get what I wanted pretty much, so when I was doing gym, it was showing. It seemed like even us looking healthy was too much for some of these racists because I didn't have shit. I'm in jail to rass, but it didn't take long before the guy in charge was giving me racist problems.

Before I got there, there were 2 guys, both white. One of them got a transfer so a position became vacant. That's when I decided to apply for it and I got it. The boss was a civilian and ex-military navy man. But he was so racist and set in his ways, he said I hadn't done something he hadn't shown me how to do. When I complained and explained this to the Race Relations Officer, he told me to stay off work while they investigated. A week later the Race Relations Officer came back to me and admitted that I was right and the guy was wrong then asked me what I wanted. I told him,

'I want an apology.'

He said, 'Look, you can have a full weeks pay and you can stay off for another week, then go back to work.' That was my apology. So when I went back the guy was pissed and you could see it. I was there smiling trying to just be cool, but he was working on a way to get me out. He finally managed to by giving me 2 Bad IEP's (Incentive Earning Privileges reports) in one day and that was me, I couldn't go back to work there. They put me back in the first job they give you when you go to prison and took my enhanced status; I was pissed. That was a good number but because I was black, they did everything they could to get me out and it worked. I had to start all over again to get another good job, but before I knew it my next problem came.

Not So Free
2009

Once a year as some kind of treat they would give us a sports day. True this was a lifer's prison it had certain things that other prisons didn't. It was like school sports for lifers. You had all kinds of events going on. On the day I didn't want to go out there with everyone, I just wanted to chill. The screws had decided to be dickheads, because we used to be able to just chill if we didn't want to get involved. But now they were telling us that it's either we go and participate in sports day, or we go to work. *Looking at the choices I obviously chose sports day.*

I went outside to look and when I saw everything going on I got involved. I had done well in high jump in another jail, so I decided to go for high jump again. It started off with 10 man, then man started licking down bars dropping out, until it ended up with 3 of us. We were all doing well, me, Omar and a next yute from Birmingham, all moving up in height until we reached about six-foot and it was my turn to jump. It was high and there was no 3rd Prize, there was only Gold and Silver, so we were all really trying. I started running fast towards the bar to get the power I needed to make the jump and that's when I heard it as I jumped. It sounded like a pencil snap, that's what man said.
I fell to the floor, my knee caps had gone up in my thighs, both my tendons snapped. They were on fire, I looked at them and it just looked like a mess. When I saw that I couldn't look again. The Screws got a stretcher and carried me off to the side of the jail, where I waited until the ambulance came. When the paramedics came they gave me gas. True I hadn't had gas before, I started off only taking a little bit. They distracted me, as they did something on my knee caps as I breathed in the gas. Then something told me to look down and that's when I saw my legs were straight again and I hadn't felt any pain. When I saw that, I sucked on that gas like a mad man, all the way to the hospital as they tended to me.

Both my legs were broken and they kicked me out the hospital after 3 days, imagine. On top of that, when I was away the Screws had started talking shit to the other inmates, man dem that I rolled with saying, 'You know that guy you roll with, he's a monster, he's in for rape.' It's like they wanted the other inmates to do me something (beat me up). They sent me back to the harsh conditions, with this new problem they had created for me and access to Doctors was only during the day. If I needed the hospital staff, I would have to wait for them to come back on duty. It was a major injury, so they should have kept me for longer, but they didn't care. When I got back on the wing, all they did was put me in a disabled cell, where I had lickle space and my lifer bredrin helped me coz I couldn't walk.

True the Screws acted like they had our best interests at heart, they put out jobs like helping other inmates and whoever did it would get an extra canteen or something. This was August 2009.

In the disabled cell it was alright, but outside the cell I had to fend for myself, like I was able bodied. Both my legs were broken. How did they expect me to do that? I had to put in a bag of complaints all the time, so I became a problem now I'm legless. With the screws telling the man dem about my charge, my same bredrin who had been helping me came and asked me about it. He was a big name in the jail, we called him the Gadget Man. One of his bredrins that I didn't know had gone to him and told him what the screws had said about me. I saw what time it was and these screws were trying to get me fixed.

I just told him straight, 'Me and her fucked, I'm not denying that, but it wasn't no rape. I went not guilty at trial, but when I got here, they told me that if I don't admit I'm guilty they wouldn't put me on the course. I had to admit guilt, or I wouldn't stand a chance of getting out.' After we talked I said, 'Furthermore, take my depositions.' I gave him all my paper work to read. I couldn't have been more upfront than that. If I was lying about anything I would never have given him all my paper work. It took about 2 weeks, but after that he came back and said 'cool.' After that I was cool, not like everyone fell in line because some of the faces in there did try to make things a little uncomfortable for me, but most were cool and the ones that weren't, didn't bring any beef to me.

The Screws had really tried to fuck me, so I had to watch them pussy holes. After that I didn't want to even communicate with them, but they still made me have to complain with how they were treating me. Then they tried to give me a bag of the nut-nut pills. The man dem on the wing that were pill experienced told me 'You see these pills; they turn man stupid, have man dribbling and shit.' I could see what man was talking about because they were fucking me up. So I went to the nurse and told her, 'These pills right here I'm not taking any more, I'll take the other ones but not these ones.'

Soon after that, the nurses were doing their check-ups on me and told me something wasn't looking right. They gave me another X-ray. Only to find out surprise surprise; with me having to fend for myself and walk, both my patellar tendons had snapped again. I had to have another operation. They were really trying to finish me off. It was a mental ting as well as a physical, but I knew I had to get out of that prison now for sure. On a positive note, I had heard from my Dad and he was trying to come and visit me.

Now I'm trying to get out of the jail, but on medical grounds they were not letting me go anywhere. They call it medical hold. They tried to draw card on me talking about, 'Well if you want to leave here, you have to show us that you can fend for yourself.' It was more of the bullshit because they moved people in wheelchair from jail to jail all the time. If they wanted to move you they could. I was trying all kinds of things to move. I got my Solicitor involved again and two twos on the day my Dad had made a bag of arrangements to finally come and visit me, a van came for me and they moved me to another jail, making me miss my Dad's visit and making him have to start that whole process again.

They moved me to Maidstone where I was meant to be able to do this next course that I needed to do. They wanted me to do some SOTP extended or the SOTP booster (Sex Offender Treatment Programme), but I had already done the SOTP core, so the other ones I was still refusing. In the end, I ended up doing a course called The Thinking Skills Programme course. It was a cognitive thinking class, only a little 2 month course, but by now I had realised that I had to play the game or I wasn't getting out. I was engaging like they wanted me to. I wasn't giving the screws any more chances to write up a bad report about me. *Just stay focussed was the way I had to see it now.*

Months later when they had decided to finished fucking with me a little bit, it was finally the day my Dad was coming with my son to visit me. It was emotional because my son at the time was 24 years old and this was the first time 3 generations of my family had been together in the same room. My Dad, my Son and me on a life sentence limping. I had to look at my life and how much of it I was missing where I was. The last time I had seen my Dad was 18 years ago when I had been on the run and when I got to the visiting room and saw him, I just cried uncontrollably for about 5 minutes. *I didn't care who saw me either*. We went through the 2-hour visit and he gave me some clothes and left me some money. After that visit I wanted to get out of jail so bad, or at least out of that prison, but at the same time I was not as fit as I used to be. I wasn't ready for road; my legs were still broken, so I couldn't move how I wanted or needed to. All I knew was I was going to think myself back to good health, positive thinking all the way. *I was dreaming I was going to walk again.*

Recovery Process

Chapter 13

I realised I definitely had to rest up. The pills they were giving me were making me constipated as well. I would sit down on the toilet sometimes for all an hour. I remember praying to God bare times. By now I decided I need to play the disabled card too, so they ended up giving me a scooter. I had to have that on file for whenever I was released. It would be easier to register on road, if I had registered in jail.

Maidstone was a nice jail for me. There was a bag of phones to use and whatever drugs I wanted. The foreigner man inside were bringing the drugs in, but infighting began pretty quickly after I got there because them man would lie and say they had paid the outside man when they hadn't, so man on the outside would refuse to send in the next parcel until they had been paid for the last one and this is where the beef started. The guy who hadn't paid, he was with my crew, but when he didn't pay the drugs obviously slowed down. With the movement of new prisoners, a new guy came in with his own links and my guy Karn tried to go connect with him, leaving us out. *Basically, he was forming another crew*. Before he was getting his drugs through visits, so it wasn't much. But this new guy had it coming over the wall, so they were getting more drugs in. *They were trying to take over.* Before we were all family, now he was trying to make a new family.

My bredrin Killer (RIP) quickly got pissed off with the fuckery Karn was keeping up with, so he decided to burn out his cell. Killer put baby oil on paper, left it on his bed and lit the match, all for switching allegiance. It burnt up in minutes, his whole life. Pictures of his wife, mum, children, phone numbers, everything he held dear to him got burnt out. After the Screws evacuated us to the fire drill spot, they went to Karn and asked him if he knew who could have started that fire and why. This is when a next man who wanted to incite violence came and whispered in man's ear, 'Killer done it.' So boom now, next thing I know I've seen the Screws marching Killer down to the block. Killer was drunk as a skunk off the jail house alcohol, hooch. He went to the block claiming his innocence and the Screws couldn't really prove it, but instead of giving him the benefit of the doubt they shipped him out. Karn ended up getting moved to another wing too and the guy that whispered in his ear came to me a few days after, while I was cutting a man's hair like, 'Yo Yanks, come here for me a minute.' He asked me if I had told Killer that he called his name, trying to draw me out. I just left him in my cell and went about my business, like I'm not entertaining it. He was trying to back it like he ain't no rat, coz he knew that if he left that one to fester on the wing, the more guys that heard and he wasn't saying anything, sooner or later it was gonna get harder for him to refute the claims. It's like he was trying to take advantage of me because I was using a walking stick and he didn't know me from when I was going on bad. He only knew me now I'm humble and trying to hold it down, especially because I couldn't really roll around with anyone in the state I was in. He started telling people that he's going to see me soon, like it's on. So, we met up in another dude's cell and started having words. Two twos he pulled out a cue stick and licked me with it across my head. I rushed him with my one leg. He's throwing punches at me and I'm throwing punches back. Two man that were in the cell with us broke it up. He left the cell first, and I followed him. The guy had hit me in the head with a cue, I was having none of it. That was a massive violation and he saw that. He ended up locking himself in his cell and didn't come out for rec or anything for the day. I was pissed outside his cell waiting for him, I'm telling him 'come out your cell. No beef!' But he wasn't on it, he was just screw-faced watching tv.

When he came out the next day, I had left it and I was chilling in a next man's cell. He came and asked if he could talk to me so I followed him to another cell and he apologised.

He said, 'Yanks, I'm sorry. I couldn't sleep all night, you're old enough to be my Dad. Could we just move on from it please.' No one on the wing liked that move because everyone knew I was cool and it was a violation, so he could feel the vibe. Man was only half talking to him, so he needed to patch that up with me before he would stop having to watch his back. So we patched that up and moved on, but soon after he got moved to another wing. *It was livelier here and it was closer to home.*

True they could see my health was getting better, they started to let me use the gym again after a year or so too. I would go from 10 til 11, 4 days a week, Monday through to Thursday and I started building back up my strength. I would ride my scooter through the wing, then park it up outside the gym and walk in with my walking stick to do my ting. Man had to respect me.

Time was ticking and the next thing for me was my parole, it was coming up soon. It was time for my town visit now where you got to walk around and interact with the public. That was a good day because it seemed like progression. It was me with these 2 funny guys, one man and one woman, but all of us in our normal clothes. They had to monitor how I interacted with people, how I used the bus, how I counted my change and how I would behave in places like McDonald's. All bullshit, but it was part of them integrating me back into society, that's what they called it. *Them watching me like an animal.*

I remember walking into McDonald's and ordering a Big Mac. I said to the wardens I was with, 'Damn, it's shrunk in the last 12 years since I've eaten one.' But I remember smiling til I must have looked mad, eating and watching people pass me by. I spent about 6 hours out there and it felt great, like I was going to be touching road soon. I walked into a sports shop and I was like a kid in a candy shop. In jail you didn't have such a variety to look at. All these things that most people take for granted, I was having to readjust to. But as I say, it was progress. The only thing with those visits was, you wasn't allowed to phone any of your people and you definitely wasn't allowed to see your family. It started to rain so the Screws suggested we go to a café, but I didn't have any more money so I told them, 'Let's just go back to the jail.' It didn't make sense me being outside standing up in the rain, just to say I'm out on road, so I went back an hour or so early. When I got back I phoned my family to tell them I was on road for the day. Then got back to prison life and continued with the motions. My son must have been excited by the thought I was getting out soon, so he sent me a letter telling me to send his sister a separate Visiting Order (VO) from his. I read between the lines assuming that maybe they wanted some time with me on their own, which I could understand.

A few weeks later my daughter came to visit me. She had just had her son. I had not only missed my grandson's birth, I didn't even know she was pregnant and she came up on her own so I didn't get to see bubba, I only heard about him. What could I say or think about that? My daughter was a woman now. I hadn't even seen her belly grow. I'm just seeing her 10 months after his birth. That was emotional. The following week my son came up, my little man was big now. As I walked in and saw him, he was sitting down next to the bree on my wing that like to dress like girl. I had to whisper the ting to my son, like, 'Yo son, you see that one wearing the dress, you know he's a man and he's not a visitor, he's an inmate on my landing. I have to see this funny guy every day.' *All of these reasons man needed to stay far from jail.* They sold condoms in jail encouraging man to turn batty man, it must be. Why else would they be giving away condoms in there, when you're with a bag of man. I really hoped my son could see how important it was for him to stay away from jail, having to see shit like that. Looking at my Son, with his full arm of tattoos and the way he was filling out his clothes. He was a man now and women on visits were even preeing (watching) him. I was proud of the man he had become, without me as well. I had given my life to the road, made bad mistakes and the punishment for that was having to sit down and watch the things I love in life move on without me. I had left him as a little footballer and now he was a body builder. *I had fucked up because all those years in the middle before he had become this man sitting down next to me were gone for ever*!

We had our visit, the 2-hour chat catching up on the last 2 years that I hadn't seen him. I told him, 'I'm trying to leave this jail to progress and I don't know when I'm getting out, but I'm hoping it's soon.' When that visit done it was all about my parole in the next few weeks. I was positive, I was thinking about my town visit, that had gone well, but they didn't even recommend any form of progression. I was so upset I couldn't even talk on my parole review. They had just looked at the fact that I refused to do the courses they wanted me to do and didn't give a shit about anything else. I didn't know how serious this IPP (Imprisoned for Public Protection) was.

When I got back on the wing, the wing Supervising Officer called me to the office and asked me if there was anything he could do. I told him, 'I just need a transfer to a prison where I can do the courses they were telling me I need to do before they will think about releasing me.' He could see that they had taken the piss and I had handled it reasonably well. He said, 'leave it with me and I'll get it sorted.' Two twos, a few weeks later a van was there to take me from Maidstone to HMP Bure. This was a full Sex Offender's jail, everyone in there was a sex offender, so there were no excuses for them to tell me that I couldn't do the courses they said I had to do. I'd been in jail this time now for 12 years; nothing in jail could surprise me now, so I just got on with it. First thing I had to do was put in an application to see someone from the Psychology Department because they were in charge of the courses. They had a little chat with me, so I told them how I'd progressed during my time in the system. They asked me how I found some of the other courses they had sent me on and because I'd been through this shit before, I knew what they needed to hear and answered accordingly. After that meeting, while I was waiting to get on the next course they suggested I start a barbering course to get my Level 1 and 2. There was a blond chick on that barbering course, that loved rubbing herself on us. It's like they sent her in there on purpose. But true my conviction, I weren't playing that game with her for a second. It could have ended badly if we had started doing a ting. *To save her skin she could have said I forced myself on her and that would have been me absolutely fucked*. I made sure I was very careful around her and I left her alone.

Within 6 months I was on the course I needed. *It was boring and dead*. All just simple common sense, but I had to do it because it was what they told me I had to do. I was never getting released if I didn't do it. The Psychologist held a lot of weight in jail and if they wrote you a good review, you could get released straight away. But if a Psychologist wrote you a bad review, you wouldn't get released unless you requested an Independent Psychologist and that Psychologist felt like the first one had been unfair. I had played this game enough to know, so I wasn't going to leave anything to chance. Before my review was scheduled, I told my Solicitor to get an Independent Psychologist that was top of the top. We met and she wrote me up a truthful report, it was real and that's how I ended up getting my D Cat to open conditions. I'd been waiting 5 years for D Cat, so as you can imagine when it came I was very happy. They sent me to HMP Leyhill Prison in Gloucester. True it was an open prison, it was constantly unlocked. Out all day basically and people are going out on home visits and day releases regular. In this jail though, the Screws were not trying to help you get released. They were aiming to get you sent back to closed conditions, by trying to draw you out. They would be quick to give you a bad report, or bad IEP (Incentive Earnings Privilege report). Anything they could do to provoke you they would try, but I wasn't taking any of their bait because all I was thinking about was my release. I needed to get out and get on with my life. I wanted my freedom back and I needed to see and spend more time with my children and grandchildren. I was getting gate happy now, this was an open prison and there was no gate to shut. I could literally walk out of this jail; so, I could taste freedom.

What happened now was, one little dickhead went out on his day release to visit the hostel he would be going to when he got released. I don't know why he decided to attack the woman that he had to meet, but he did and that fucked up all of us on a ripple effect ting. *That made me actually check myself and some of the ripple effects I might have caused with some of my actions over the years.* All of our privileges got taken for 6 weeks because of that and where I was supposed to get my day release after 4 months, I had to wait 9 months before I finally got mine. I went to Bristol Town Centre on that day release. It was me and one screw and the day went well. We got off at the bus garage and went to a café. It was the first time I had gone to a café in 15 years to order a breakfast. After I ate that we headed to the library. I went on their computers then we left and went to a Job Centre. It was a reality check for me even in there now because it had changed since the last time I was there too. You had Security Guards greeting you at the door asking you "how can they help." You had laptops now and you sent emails to employers instead of using the cards and phoning up like you had in the old days. It was a half day release so after we had done that, it was time to go back to jail. I had to write a report about my day out and the Screw had to write a report on what she thought about how I handled it. She wrote a good report, that meant that I could now go out on my own. That was a next progression going out on a home leave. I just had to do 2 more town visits on my own. That gate happy feeling was all over my body now. I did one and it went well, then 2 days before I was due to do my last town visit, they caught me smoking in my cell. They had implemented this new no smoking in your cell policy only a month before. It wasn't even a blanket ban on all jails. They were just trying it out in certain jails, so they had certain man all shook to smoke a roll up in their cell like they are smoking drugs. Anyway, they fucked me over. I wasn't able to go on my last town visit and they sent me back to a C Cat closed condition jail, Gloucester Prison to be lost in the system.

They banged me up with a 22-year-old yute from South London first. He was a calm yute, ahead of his time, so we could work even though I was back in the grime of bang up and all the other bullshit. I knew I had fucked up, so I didn't make any noise about it. I started gyming it with my cell mate and they gave me a little ratings because of the weight I could push. In all I spent about 3 weeks in there, I kept my head down and started writing in a diary about my thoughts and feelings. After those 3 weeks a van came for me and took me from Gloucester to Lincoln prison for a night. They put me in the segregation instead of just putting me on the mains, for my safety they said, but it was just easier for them. Easy in and easy out, but this cell they put me in was so dirty I couldn't even take my clothes off and sleep good. *It wasn't that type of party.* The next day they moved me on, finally back to HMP Bure. Where they took my picture again. This time when they took my picture I smiled. These pussies would have expected me to be all the way down, but I had seen over the years they marked down everything from in the prison van, to these reception visits, to when you socialise with other inmates, to all the other little things. So I wanted to show them I could deal with this. Later on I could say I would be able to cope with adversity.

When I got back into the HMP Bure life, the Psychologists brought me in for a talk. I shared my thoughts with them and they decided to get me sent back to the D Cat prison, but I told them, 'No I don't want to go back to the D Cat thank you.' It doesn't do what it says on the tin. In all the time I'd been in this prison system, I'd seen the D Cat do the opposite of what it was supposed to do. A bag of people had been sent back to C Cat. The Screws had tried to give bad reports and all kind of other things, to hinder a man's progress.

I told them, 'I'd prefer to stay right here until my release' and when they saw that they knew I was serious. I had finally seen that D Cat was a fake privilege.

The last 5 months was a nightmare, I didn't know whether I was coming or going. On top of the fact they had me in a 2 man cell with a bag of funny brees. First, they put me with a man that snored loud all night. So loud I couldn't even sleep. I had to sleep in with him for a few nights, then they put me with a young dude who suffered from depression. All he wanted to do was take medication and sleep. He had been recalled a bag of times and he didn't want to learn anything. The next guy they brought to share with me was an ex-army guy. This guy had been caught for an offence 25 years later because of improvements in DNA. True he was an ex-army guy, he had a better relationship with the Screws because they kind of see army guys like themselves. The first day we were talking he said 'Yeah, I killed a few people. I actually liked it!' I wondered why he was telling me that, maybe he wanted me to think something of him or see a certain face, but by that time I was just trying to get the fuck out, so I didn't care too much even though I did have to think about what he was telling me. *Man's telling me he liked to kill ya na.* So anyway, I was trying to respect his space and just co-exist, but it was difficult. First of all, he would keep the light on until all times of night, reading. Then one night I'm trying to sleep and all I can hear is this man scratching. I heard it and wondered what he was scratching for so long, til I looked up to see. When I turned on the light and looked at him, he was scratching his leg, but where he was on the top bunk, all his dead skin was falling off his bed and landing on mine. That was a fucking problem, but I still tried to hold it down. The last straw was when I went out to rec and came back to see this guy had taken my mattress off my bed frame and put it on the floor, so he could stand on it and do whatever he was doing to his bed. The guy fixed up his bed and had the cheek to leave my mattress on the floor. He didn't even fix mine back, so I wouldn't notice. I decided that I needed to think about how to handle this because I knew they were gonna give me a bad report if I didn't handle it properly. When he came back I talked to him calm. I didn't want him to feel like I was putting it on him in any way, but he saw an angle. He wanted a single cell like I did, so he went to the screws and told them I was bullying him. This made the screws come to me talking about its not looking good for me, I've had 3 people in my cell in the last 3 months and each of them have left in a hurry. They asked me if I'm sure I'm not bullying people. They put me on bully watch for 8 weeks and left the bully watch on my head even when they moved me to a new wing. I was happy about that because at least now I didn't have to stay in the cell with that guy. But at the same time, I had to hold it down 100%, or I would have been in big trouble.

After about 2 months guess who I see on my new wing? The

same guy! It's like they wanted something to happen with me and him because I couldn't understand, if after they know we have a little history, why would they put us back in the same vicinity. On top of the fact that on this new wing I knew everyone so if I wanted him to get touched, I wouldn't have even had to do it myself. They were definitely trying something because they didn't give me a job. They were doing everything they could to wind me up, but I wasn't biting on any of it. They were supposed to give me a barber job, but they lost the application. It was ok though because I always found a way.

This was the wing I was on when I went for my last parole review, June 2016. This was my chance and I wasn't going to waste this one. I didn't even let my solicitor talk. I gave them a little bit of Psychology, along with their language and a little bit of street, just so they knew I wasn't acting, but this talk I gave them came from the Most High. Everyone was shocked with what I was telling them. I had had enough of this system and I was making sure they couldn't see any reason why I might need to stay in there any longer. When I finished with them I could see I had made a good impression. I had every bit of paperwork they had asked me to do and more. I had a bag of good reports now and I wasn't taking any bait. They told me that I would hear from then in 14 days' time, but I didn't hear from them. The Parole Board sent a recommendation to all the other people that was involved in my case to change their recommendation from D Cat to release. After that talk I had given them they had wanted to release me, but some of the others like the Screws didn't want me to go, so they had tried to fuck me, but the Parole Board was the final say and whatever it said went. Everybody had to jump to that tune there.

This was in July. I was supposed to have my answer in 14 days like they said, but they were dragging their feet until October, when they told me I was going to be released. Finally, but I still had to wait another month until they released me. I learnt the day I was getting released a week before the day which was the November the 9th.

They dragged their feet all the way out to the day. Considering inmates are supposed to be released in the morning. I packed up all my shit from the night before, 15 years of jail life. I gave bare tings to the man dem, clothes, clippers and all kind of other tings. There were things I gave away I wished I didn't, but I was leaving and them man wasn't. I was ready to leave from morning, but they had me locked up like I was still an in mate til afternoon, still going servery on my day of release to eat. Trust me, you ain't out of that system until you out. But the paperwork finally got done and they let me out of those doors in Norwich. They got me a cab to the station, a 45-minute drive, then from there a 2 hour train ride to Liverpool Street where I waited for my son to come and pick me up. The fast life was in my face; people everywhere with no time to stop, business people doing their ting and all that. I was looking up and down for my son, but I couldn't see him. I decided to get some change to phone him, so I kneeled down to go in my bags and as I was looking I heard, 'Yo stranger!' It was my son. I looked up and saw this big man standing in front of me.

Freedom

Chapter 14

It was a big embrace, then he helped me with one of my bags and we jumped on a train to Walthamstow Central. He showed me where he got his trim. The barber knew me from before he knew my son, so now he was seeing us both together it was nice all around. I could see how much things had changed in the time I'd been away and the change was shocking, trust me. After that we headed to Chingford where I went and saw his mum and my daughter. We had a little chat for an hour or so, then I had to kick back to my hostel in Brixton before curfew. They had me like a kid, setting my curfew for nine in the evening. But this is what happens when you give your life to the system. My Probation Officer wanted to see me on the day of my release too. She even went to Brixton, but they understood it was impossible because I had left jail so late. So we arranged in the evening to meet up the following day in Walthamstow Court House, where the Probation Office was. The next day as I was travelling to probation, I came out of Walthamstow and saw my daughter getting her hair done in the hairdresser. We hadn't made any arrangements to meet on that day, but obviously from she saw me we were rolling. I couldn't believe how my daughter had grown, she had her daddy proud. We travelled to the probation together where I met my probation officer. She was a very sexy chick, you know the type that you are happy to see and she didn't go in on me for not meeting her the day before. I think it was because I was with my big woman daughter and I remember her saying, she would have liked to also meet my son because he had corresponded with her a lot when I was inside. Probation asked me how I was feeling to be out and she told me, due to cut backs I couldn't get access to the Gym which was a stress reliever for me. I just had to deal with that. I can't lie though, they had me walking on egg shells; it was one pussy hole Screw that had told me "you'll be back", trying to draw me out one day. I wasn't trying to ever go back. From there now, because my probation was in Walthamstow I would try and hang around until everyone came back from work, so I could see my children and baby mother. I was trying to rebuild my life, true so much time had been lost. The curfew ting was long, but that was another part of my conditions and if I broke that, they could easily recall me back to prison and the hostel was an extension of jail watching me. I couldn't even smoke in my room. If they caught you more than once, recall. A next term of my probation was I had to take a drug test every week. They had me living like a boy with all these things to watch out for, on top of all the other conditions I had to abide by. They call this hostel an Approved Premises. In a normal hostel, you wouldn't have to live by these rules, but when you come out of jail, this is where they send you, hoping you step out of line so they can recall you. If they really wanted rehabilitation, they would make better use of taxpayer's money. Imagine, I had to show that I had support on road and recommendations for a job, which I did, as a youth facilitator. But on top of everything they were putting me through, when I got out ready to start working, they told me I couldn't do that and they wanted me to go the Job Centre route. Everyone loses in this except for the system, they eat while we starve. They wanted me to struggle and see how I coped with that, no push, they wanted to hold me. Lead me into depression. I had someone offering me a good job, trying to rehabilitate the yutes, but they were telling me I couldn't do that. What would they expect me to do, other than fall into depression? The system is not fit for purpose on purpose. All the rules they put in place are put there hoping that you will do something that needs another punishment. It's all a big scam.

The Job Centre route that they encouraged me to go down, wasn't even set up for me as it should have been. So, I started to fall behind on my rent. I ended up having to borrow money to postpone my eviction. I had a job offer I'm not allowed to do, they force me to go Job Centre, they don't set up my tings properly, then leave me with nothing when I'm getting eviction notices. This is something else I could get recalled for. In a normal hostel you would just get kicked out, in this hostel I could get sent back to prison if they wanted to. They had me stressing and when I went to my probation and express my fears, the probation told me, 'Nah we wouldn't just recall you like that.' But I knew the shady fuckery the hostels and probations could keep up with, spending so much time in jail. *I remembered one guy coming back to jail on a recall ting, telling me he had been in one of these hostels and the manager of the hostel had forced him to wash his car and sweep up around the premises. Absolutely nothing to do with his release conditions and when he had refused to do it, he had been recalled.* That was living proof because we were rubbing shoulders in jail, so I wasn't trusting anything they said. I always tried to, but they always did something that showed me they weren't to be trusted. They would put it down to they're just doing their job, but this was my life and I had to move smart now.

Life had changed on the outside in 15 years. The mobile phones was the biggest single change. People were socialising on their phone now, where before people would socialise with each other. Now people's lives seemed to be in their phone. If you asked someone a question, you would get a funny look now, until you had finished your sentence. It was hard for me to get back into the swing of things with all of this to contend with. Everyone with a friendly face had moved on, some for better and some for worse. I had to solider on, I couldn't dwell on it but I noticed. Everything changed and I just had to catch up. Slowly I started linking back with some of my old guys, the ones that were alright and I wouldn't get recalled for hanging around with.

My old bredrin Fixer had managed to get my number, so one evening when I was going back to the hostel he gave me a call. I

answered wondering who it was because not many people had the number. It was good to hear from him still and we made arrangements to link up the following day. We linked at his Dad's yard and reasoned for a little, but I couldn't chill for long because I had to get back to the hostel. He called another blast from the past to come link us, but he didn't tell me, so when I saw this SUV pull up and Fixer told me to get in, I just thought it was a cab, but when man turned around to say wha gwan and I caught his eye, we had to get out of the car to greet each other properly. It had been a long time; so, we talking as we roll, me, Fixer and Richard. We were on our way to look for a next bredrin, Rebel. As we got to Higham Hill Road, I saw him. I had to jump out on him too. Another friendly face I hadn't seen for a minute (very long time). We were there talking when I looked down the road and saw a guy that looked like Maskey, but I didn't think it was him because man had told me he's wasn't on the ends any more. But when I looked again it really was Maskey, so now I had a good few man that I hadn't seen for at least 15 years. Some of them hadn't even seen each other, then out of nowhere I saw Tyrone. Wow, that was a big day and that made me know I'm back.
What I had to think about was, now they had put the brakes on me trying to help the yutes, what was I going to do with my life. I had a few offers for barber shops, but due to my knee problem, I wasn't going to be able to do that. On top of the fact that they wanted to offer me just 2 days a week work. I had left road a big man, but it seemed like the system didn't want me coming back a big man. The system wanted me to come back looking and feeling like a boy, so that I would need their "SO CALLED SUPPORT."

This Feels Like Prison

I had a lot of regrets and I had missed a lot of time that I couldn't get back. Seeing my children's children for the first time and being uncomfortable around them, was a very horrible feeling. The system had almost brainwashed me into feeling like maybe I shouldn't be around my grandchildren because if they say I'm an animal, maybe I really am. I had to just be quiet and smile as I watched them in amazement. Then watching my son be a dad. To watch him amazed me again, he was the dad I wished I could be. *Just seeing him be the man he was made me proud.* He was in good shape, working, looking after his boy as he was supposed to and like I wished I had. Then there was my other daughter, Chelsea. I didn't know where to start with her. Me and her mum had not made the right foundation for her because we were not able to. It wasn't anyone's fault but our own and I knew 25 years later, it was always going to be a hard conversation to have. I didn't know how I could make something like that up to her, but I wanted to. It was all about rebuilding. That's the way I saw it, but because she lived so far from me and I didn't have any money, I just felt like it would be best if I stayed away until I fixed up. I didn't know how I was going to fix up as a 50-year-old Man with no real prospects, but I was going to try even though it's like the system wanted me to be a waste man now for the rest of my life.

My plan became to get my place and get work. I had a few friends that wanted to help me, but I at least needed a CSCS card. That would have given me the ability to become a labourer. That was something I should have done in jail, but because I was moved out of D Cat, I had missed the opportunity to do the course. I could have done it during a day release, but now I was out of jail, they were telling me I would need to do my CSCS course in probation. I decided to do it still, so they had me in probation for 4 days training Health and Safety CSCS. That would at least get me on site. I was doing the training, but because it wasn't a one on one and people were talking all the time, I couldn't take it in. Obviously because I'm an ex-con, there wasn't going to be any special treatment for me. So when it came time for me to take the test, I failed. I felt useless! People were banking on me to pass that and I was so confident I would. I told everyone I was going to pass and now I had to tell them I had failed. It wasn't a good feeling. But where I had breath, I had hope. I knew I had to keep trying until I succeeded. I had to stay positive and I stayed positive by keeping positive people around me.

One evening a long time bredrin came into my mind named Blacks. He was one of my younger bredrin's I always had love for. I wondered what he was on. I phoned him and that's when he asked me, 'Yo Yanks, you want to write a book about your life.' Without a second thought I said, 'YES!' I slept peaceful that night. I wondered if this could be my chance to tell my story and hopefully inspire someone to see the error of their ways before they ended up like me, or even worse. The next day I spoke to Blacks again and he told me who I needed to meet and that it wouldn't be easy, but if I put in the work, it would get done. I had faced a lot in my life, so I wasn't expecting anything moving forward to be easy, but I knew I needed to give something back. I had a lot of important eyes on me now, like my children and grandchildren. I didn't want to live with anymore regrets. I needed to earn their respect because I didn't have it. How could I, when I had missed so many important years of their lives. I had made many bad decisions and I had no one to blame for what had happened to me but myself. Many people throughout my life had said to me that I should write a book, but it all just sounded like a myth.

Blacks was my bredrin and I trusted him. When he brought me an opportunity like this I grabbed it with both hands. I started feeling optimistic because I knew that was the way forward. Blacks gave me the number I needed to call and I linked the guy a few weeks after we initially talked. It was a summer afternoon when I met Sibs, the guy that was going to help me give something back to the community. He invited me to an event on police brutality, where they were protesting about the death of another black youth in police custody. Sibs had his books and as I watched him sell to almost everyone he spoke to, I had visions of that maybe being me one day. He was with a next author named Sherlock who had another story that I could relate to. The journey began to look realistic. It took me another week or so to link Sibs again and start the actual writing. The first day I got to his house we started talking and getting it down. After a few hours we had made a real start. I had a lot to say and I could see it was going to be a long journey, but one that had to be done. We had a long way to go, but we had started.

Life went on in the meantime and probation had stopped me from taking the first job I had been offered, working as a Mentor. I was deflated about that. I thought about getting back into crime and the drugs game because everything was long, but I had to take my license seriously. They would have happily taken me back to jail and that would have defeated the whole object of me telling my story. I held down my negative thoughts and focused on the book. I had to keep thinking of the bigger picture.

There were a few people that I had wanted to see when I got out, that I hadn't linked up with yet. Wayne was one of them, I classed him as a bredrin from back in the day, but everyone I had spoken to about him hadn't seen him. I wondered wha gwan and figured I'd link up with him sooner or later. Sibs didn't stop surprising me, when he called me out of the blue one day to ask me if I knew Wayne. They were not in the same circle, so I wondered how they had linked. Apparently, Sibs had told one of his youngers that he was helping me with my book and his younger remembered me from back in the day. He remembered I used to roll with Wayne so this is how he made the link. I was happy to hear from Wayne, if just to see how 15 years had treated him. I didn't know what to expect. We talked on the phone and arranged to link up. In between working on the book, a lot of negative people would try to divert me from my goal. When I saw them, they would ask me what I was doing now I'm out and I would tell them I'm working on my book. They wouldn't really have anything positive to say about that and this made me see who I needed to spend my time with. I had realised that, if you want to be successful, you had to surround yourself with successful people. If I spent my time with scum bags, I was only going to end up doing the same things that led to all that jail time. Those people made me focus more and I started seeing my story take shape. It was happening faster than I thought and there was one day when I stayed with Sibs longer than normal and we really got a lot done. *I saw how close I was to my dream*. Imagine in all this, I would have expected probation to be happy for me or encourage me at least, but it seemed like they weren't too happy with my progress either. It all started with them asking me if I was lonely. I hadn't even thought about it before they asked me. It's like they were trying to feel me out and see where my mind was. But as they planted the seed, I did start feeling like it would be nice to get myself a girlfriend.

Over the next few weeks I went out looking and ended up finding a nice girl called Alishia. She lived far away though, so I couldn't see her as often as I would have liked. But as I got to know her better and she would tell me about where she lived, I started feeling like maybe I could actually live with her. The cost of living was a lot cheaper and it would have been like a new start for me.

True I wanted to stay above board with the probation and the terms of my release was, I had to tell them about any girlfriend I had. I told them about her, on top of the fact that most people around me were not on my new page. I thought they would have been glad I was thinking about making those big steps to better my life, but probation showed me their other face in an instant. Up until this point they had been showing me their alright face, but the minute I told them about my new relationship, they started some other shit. I've left jail almost a year now, but they still want to tell me when I can jump. I had to give them all my girl's contact information and they called her straight away. The conversation consisted of them trying to talk her out of being with me. They asked her about 3 times if she knew I had been convicted of rape, after I had obviously told her and I had told them that I had told her. I had to wonder what their motives for me really were. Did they want rehabilitation? It didn't seem like it, it was like they wanted to push me into reoffending, so they could recall me. It was all a trick; the system was working just the way it was supposed to for them. They take taxpayers money to house prisoners, overcharge the taxpayer then encourage ex-convicts to go on this course and that course, so the prison system can make more money. The ex-cons get nothing out of it and are left to find our own way in society. This is why it was so important for me to tell my story, all of it.

A Lesson Learned and Realisation That I will Never Be Free

I'm 51 years old now and my IPP finishes long after I will be dead and gone. In the meantime the probation can tell me when I need to see them, what I can and can't do for life and if I step out of line enough, they will send me back to jail. I need everyone to know, what I did was wrong and I deserved punishment. I've put my life on a plate for everyone to see, but also what I'm going through and believe me it's not nice. If I can encourage one person to change a negative path to a positive one, then I've done what I intended to. After spending a total of 23 years in jail, friendly faces I remembered before I left are hard to find. Life doesn't wait for any of us and when you decide to act first without thinking, the system's got you. No one will be waiting for you when you get out. I'm talking from experience because I can tell you, when I came out things weren't the way they were when I left them, everything had changed. I was lucky I got the opportunity to do this, turn my life around and have the chance to make my children proud of me. But who knows, I still might be too late.

All you wanna be bad boy's, learn your books. There will come a time in all your lives, where you regret what you've done if you live that long. Learn from other people's mistakes. Don't let that big jail sentence be your lesson. The system will happily watch you waste away in there. Be the support you needed in life, it's just as easy to affect people positively. It just takes a little bit more imagination.

Message From Mummy

And just to set the record straight because it had been playing on my mind for years, my Mum moved to Barbados so I couldn't just go and see her and ask so I phoned her to ask,

'Mum, my Dad said that when I was a baby, you turned on the gas and tried to kill me in the house, is that true?'

'No Mark, your Dad is lying again, you were sleeping, and it was cold outside. I needed to get you some food at the shop, just down the road and I didn't want to wake you and take you out in it. I thought I had turned on the heater, but the flint didn't light it properly. I went to the shop and came back and smelt the gas. I grabbed you and ran outside, so you could get some fresh air.

I told your Dad about that, he wasn't even there. He was to busy fucking around with all his women, so you don't listen to your dads lies son. I love you now as I loved you then and I always will.'

SPECIAL PREVIEW

A Product of My Environment

Chris Sibia

LONDON'S finest

London's Finest Distribution
London, UK

www.LondonFinestDistribution.com

Info@LondonsFinestDistribution.com

Chapter 1

The first thing he said when I answered the phone was, 'Chris, the police are coming for you!'

'Why you say that bruv?' I asked.

'I just got out of the police station and I had to give them your name, or they would have recalled me back to jail.'

'FUCK! What did you tell them?'

'I told them they need to talk to you because I don't know anything, I'm letting you know so you can tidy your yard for when they come cos they're coming.'

'Ok!' *I couldn't be to pissed off with him even though he had ratted me out because of the circumstances*. But, it was all too much with everything else that was going on in my life so I jumped in the whip (car) and rolled out to stay with my Country chick, Bianca. She rolled out the red carpet for me and I loved every minute of it. She was an amazing cook, I loved the way she put it on me and I was far from all the mess I was in, so I could relax.

I stayed at Bianca's for as long as I could and trust me, I did not want to leave even though I felt guilty. Bianca didn't know Sherena was pregnant and Sherena didn't know Bianca was pregnant. *Pressure*! In the end I decided I had to go home because I knew boy dem were coming and I remembered there was some paper work I had forgotten to move that I needed to.

I felt like crying when I said, 'Bye.'

It's true she had made me feel so comfortable, on top of the fact I didn't know what I was going home to.

When I got back to the ends me and Sherena still weren't even talking. She had made her decision to have our baby and I couldn't do fuck all, other than accept it. *I was just glad I had convinced Bianca to terminate hers.*

I was a womanizer and I hadn't seen anything wrong with what I was doing in all honesty, until they had both hit me with the pregnant talk. This was why I was in half the problems I was in and it seemed like my problems had no end because that was just the half of them.

I had another chick I was fucking with at the time who lived across the road from my yard. I stayed at her yard most nights when I was on the ends and I'm not gonna lie, I loved sleeping at North Wezzys house. I was able to see any mess from a distance and if I needed to walk past my house like a passer-by, I could.

Each day I touched road to go home, I looked out cautiously and was surprised the boy dem hadn't come for me yet. Sherena and this baby situation was playing on my mind. I didn't know what was happening, or how she was. I was in a real mess and even man like Francis wasn't talking to me all now. I was a liability, I could see it myself!

I probably would have thought that too if I had a guy around me that kept fucking up my shit, making a bag of mess, after all I'd ever tried to do was help him.

Nothing happened for about a week when I got back. Then my brother got sucked off (arrested) by Luton boy dem. A little trail had found its way back to him, so they got him as part of their investigation. He gave them a no comment interview. *We knew it was coming, so it wasn't a surprise.*

I just wanted to know how much they knew, but by the time he got out and came back to the ends, he didn't seem bothered by what they had on him. The fact he weren't bothered made me comfortable because if they didn't have much on him, they weren't gonna have much on me and I was going to make them work to get me too. *I wasn't putting anything on a plate for them pussy holes.*

I still hadn't spoken to Sherena weeks later. I justified my behavior by telling myself, she was keeping up with fuckery, having our baby.

She was about six months gone when she finally called to tell me, 'Something's wrong Chris, you need to come to the hospital now.'

I didn't know what was wrong but I knew I had to go. So I made my way to meet her. When I got there, the doctors told me that Sherena had gone into premature labour and they were sending her to Homerton Hospital, which at the time had the only premature unit in East London.

It was a lot! My brain started racing, wondering if anything I'd done had contributed to this. I had done a lot and right now I just had to try and be as supportive as possible.

We got to Homerton about an hour later and Sherena was given an epidural where after a few hours of labour she had our baby Kayan. It was emotional – Bubba was so tiny. As soon as he came out, Sherena just bursted into tears, maybe because Bubba wasn't crying and she knew something was wrong. I didn't know what to do with myself.

Sherena's friend told me, 'Hug her Chris, just hug her.'

I didn't know if she wanted me to, but after her friend said that I gave Sherena a hug and a kiss and told her, 'Everything will be alright.' Then I turned to the doctor working on our baby, he had a few nurses around him.

After a few minutes, the doctor lifted his head and said, 'Erm, I'm sorry. Your baby's dead!'

Erm, my baby's dead. The sentence twirled around in my head for a minute. It was a moment of shock and disbelief mixed in with anger at the casual way he said it. I was thankful there was a midwife there that cared. I didn't want to make it racial, but couldn't help notice she was black.

With compassion she said, 'No he's not, we're going to try with this baby.' Looking at the doctor as she pumped air into his little lungs.

I looked at that doctor, thinking are you fucking stupid? You just said my baby's dead and he's not! I gave him a look that said, you better save my baby's life you little prick or I'm going to do you something for dem massive lies.

That pussy got it and got to working on my bubba. Tough guy needed help. There were a lot of things wrong with him being born so premature. He weighed 660 grams and some of his internal organs weren't developed properly. On the outside, he looked normal, just very small but he wasn't.

We went back to Sherena's that evening to get some bits and get ready for what might be a long stay, with a lot of sleepless nights and something told me to pick up one of her books. I originally picked it up to ask her why she wastes her time reading this shit, but I read the first page and it actually got me.

In the two weeks tough guy spent in Homerton Hospital I saw it all. I saw my baby turn blue. I saw parents go crazy on staff and after all the neglect I saw them keeping up with in there, I knew if our baby stood any chance of surviving, he had to leave that hospital. The pussy hole doctor had already lied and told me my baby was dead, so I had to wonder how much they were trying.

One afternoon I just decided to cotch (chill) and sit with little man talking to him and watching him sleep. I'd taken out the book that I took from Sherena's house, *A Piece of Cake,* to have a little read when little man had fallen asleep. I must have been there quiet for so long the nurses forgot I was there.

Being at the hospital every day, I'd learnt what some of the different-colour lines and noises on the machines meant. An incubator across the room started going nuts. There were four nurses in the room, just chatting amongst themselves. The machine was making all kinds of noises, telling them the baby needed attention now or the baby's gonna die. Almost a minute passed, with me wondering how are they still standing up chatting. I poked my head around the corner for them to see me, then they jumped into action, like *oh shit, we forgot about him*. I just shook my head and thought about all the times I'd not been there, all the time my baby had been left with these fake nurses. That same neglect right there was probably the reason my baby had turned blue.

I told Sherena, 'Yo, we have to get him out of here, they don't give a shit about our baby and I'm gonna go nuts on someone round here soon.'

A few days after that, little man was transferred to Royal London Hospital.

This was an older hospital with equipment that didn't seem up-to-date like the shit in Homerton, but the nurses made me comfortable that little man was there with them. It felt like they cared and that's what little man needed. It was still 50/50 whether he was going to make it, but in Homerton it felt like the chances was next to nothing.

I spent my days just chilling with him, holding his hand and talking to him and when he was sleeping I'd read more of *A Piece of Cake*. The thing with this book that kept me reading were the things the author, Cupcake Brown, went through. As I read, I wondered how come I was even reading her book. It amazed me that she'd been through all that and come out the other end and had written a book about it.

Me and Sherena had been by his side every day now for a

month and it seemed like little man was getting bigger. I had built my bond with little man. He was my soldier and I told him he needed to be strong because I wanted to see him playing with his big brothers.

He would even hold my hand like he knew who I was when I put my hand in to play with him.

On the last day I got there, I could see the water marks from his eyes on his face, he'd been crying. That wasn't good. With all that morphine they'd given him, I never wanted to see him cry! I felt like anytime I saw him cry he didn't want to fight any more.

The doctor came in shortly after we got there and asked us if he could talk to us as he closed the curtain around us and little man. I looked at Sherena as she looked at me. I knew this wasn't something I wanted to hear. We looked at the doctor. The doctor explained Kayan hadn't been toilet since he'd been born. His kidneys just weren't working and that's what was killing him. I started to cry. He had made me proud, a big month he'd lived, after that pussy hole in Homerton told me he was dead.

Now this doctor was telling us, 'We've tried everything for him but nothing's working. We're going to turn off his life support machine and give him some dignity in his death if he doesn't show any improvement by this evening.'

At this point me and Sherena just held each other and cried uncontrollably, for everyone to hear. All families with their premature babies, knew what those tears were for. I knew they were just happy it was someone else getting bad news. *I had to get out of there*

The doctor said he was going to leave him for one last day just to make sure, but I knew the next time I was in that hospital they were going to be letting our baby die.

As we left, all eyes were on us. I didn't want anyone's pity, I just wanted my baby to live and come home so we could watch him grow like his older brothers.

Chapter 2

The drive home was quiet and resigned. I had been a bastard and I didn't want to live with any more regrets. I had too many already and I felt responsible for this. It was early evening and it took hours to get home because of all the traffic. We decided to eat something and get an early night, because it was going to be a long and horrible few days.

We hadn't been sleeping more than two hours when we got a call from a nurse, talking about, 'Kayan's getting worse and we don't think he's going to make it through the night.' She told us, 'Come now and be with him in his final hours.'

That phone call was emotional! They were basically telling us to come and watch our baby die. We got ready and we were there in about half an hour, true there was hardly any traffic. We sat with him as his heart rate slowly got weaker and weaker. His skin was falling off in front of us and I was trying to be strong, but I was crying like a little girl.

Then finally came the point where the nurse took us into a bedroom and brought him in, morphine attached, to be with us for his last hour. That was the first time we'd been able to hold him since he'd been born. He was so tiny, even holding him was difficult. Sherena held him for a bit, then I held him, til he died in my arms.

The nurse came in a little while later and told me he's definitely gone now, but I didn't want to let go even though I saw he was gone in his eyes.

She took him, leaving us with pictures and broken hearts. We'd been with him for the whole night and now it was coming on to 7 in the morning. As we left and got in the car we see some scavenging ticket warden pussy holes hanging around waiting for the clock to strike 7, so they could start ticketing people's cars.

Driving home that morning, the tears were rolling down my face like a running tap. I didn't care who saw me. I hadn't cried for years and everyone who saw me that morning knew what I was crying for. A man like me only cried like that for death.

It was time for bed when we got home. We needed time to gather our thoughts and rest, so we slept for a few hours.

Later we were up and hungry, with no food in the fridge. I wanted some curry goat, so it was all about that little spot in Wood Green. We jumped in the whip to go get some food.

What we didn't know was, that morning, when we were travelling home, a boy dem (police) from Wood Green station had been stabbed to death – and when boy dem get murdered on the ends, they go hard on everybody til the person who did it gets caught. That's why as we were driving, there was so much boy dem on road. It was problematic for me because I knew they had warrants out for my arrest. I was bait and I knew the next time the boy dem stopped me they were trying to take me to jail. Today wasn't the day I was trying to go to jail though – no fucking way. So I was trying to get in and out real quick.

As we got to the food spot, a boy dem caught us turning on to a side road to park and blue-lighted us.

I thought, look at this right now.

They told us the reason they stopped us was because it had come up on the system that the car didn't have insurance.

It's a good thing Sherena had decided to drive.

They told her she needed to get blah, blah, blah, but for now they were taking the car.

The pussy holes didn't even care about our situation. I felt to whack him in his jaw, but if I had done that I knew it was going to get on top quickly. When you're backed into corners, you do funny things. But he was giving me the opportunity to bounce, so I took it.

I told Sherena, 'I'm going to get a cab for us.'

The boy dem hadn't asked me my name yet and I didn't know I didn't have to give them my name if I hadn't done anything wrong. I felt like he was going to ask me sooner or later, so I decided to bounce before he did.

I phoned her and told her, 'Get the food and jump in a cab, I'll pay for it when you get home.'

She knew why I had to bounce, the whole situation was bad. But it was either I bounce and be with her for the evening, or I risk hanging around and it gets on top.

That evening, after I'd spent lickle time with Sherena, I went back to the ends to see man dem. I ended up at Justin's, chilling with Justin, Jamma, Spray, Blacks and a few other man. We talked about my lickle man. He was gone and I couldn't believe it. *Crazy*!

I spent a few days with Sherena, then it was time to break the bad news to little Lamar and Rocharne. I hadn't let them meet their little brother because I wasn't sure if he was going to make it and I knew if they saw him the attachment would have been stronger and it would have made a bad situation worse.

I went and told Lamar first, true he was the big brother. I wasn't sure if he was going to understand, but little man never stopped surprising me with his knowledge.

As I told him, he fell to pieces. Then he stopped crying for a minute to ask me, 'Are you joking Dad?'

How could I joke about something like that, shit was serious.

Lamar cried with me for about an hour straight. I really didn't think it would have affected him the way it did. It made me recognize he was a big boy. I took Lamar with me down to Rocharne's and we broke the news to him.

Rocharne took it how I thought Lamar would. He didn't really feel it the same way, thankfully. I made sure they hadn't met Kayan for that exact reason, but Lamar cried like I would have expected him to cry for Rocharne. It was touching!

I decided to bring them down to London with me to spend time while we sorted out the funeral arrangements. I let everything else just go over my head. I didn't care about anything other than getting past the funeral.

The day was finally here. Justin scooped me and the yute mans in the morning. It was a week day and early morning, so I understood some man couldn't make it due to work and other commitments – but man with funny excuses showed themselves, even though I knew who was who already.

After the funeral, we went and had lunch. It was one of those days I wanted behind me.

The little guys had been with me for a few days now and they needed to get back to school so I decided to chill with Sherena for the rest of the day til evening, go back to mine and sleep, then take the yute mans back early morning. Maybe they could go school half day or something. But the next morning things didn't go quite to plan.

Chapter 3

I needed to get something for their breakfast and handle some business, so we headed over to the market. As I finished handling my business and we were going to get the food, two undercover boy dem stopped me out of nowhere.

'Chris Sibia, we're arresting you on suspicion of blah blah. You do not have to say anything, but it may harm your defence if you do not mention something you later rely on in court. Anything you do say can and will be used in evidence against.'

All I could do was laugh. I knew it was coming, but I would never have guessed it would have been today.

Lamar asked them if they were joking. He was really growing into a man. Like me, he couldn't believe my luck.

Then both Lamar and Rocharne fell to pieces and just started bawling, out of control.

Lamar said, 'My Dad ain't hurt nobody! Why don't you go catch some real criminals and let us mourn in peace? We just buried my little brother yesterday! What's wrong with you people? Leave us alone!'

The boy dem told him, 'Your Dad's just going to help us with our enquiries,' and when my little mans saw I was cool, they calmed down.

Then them pussy holes asked me if there was anyone the little mans could stay with because it was going to take a while.

I told them, 'No! I'm taking them home to Luton and Bedford, unless you want to drop them first.'

They weren't on that like I thought. I told them I needed to get my car out of the car park too and take it home, so they let me do that as well. I had to drive my car home with this undercover up inside and the next one in a car following behind me.

We got to my yard, then they started searching for evidence and taking my shit. They took everything they could find and it's a good thing I had got my important stuff out as I knew they were coming. They still found some stuff in my house I had forgotten about, but they knew they had to take me seriously when they saw some of the books I had lying around.

I had started applying covert hypnosis on them as soon as they arrested me, building fake rapport. By now, my little guys were relaxed and going through the motions with me. They were a next set of country boy dem investigating me, so they were taking me country too. After they finished searching my yard, they put us in the car to take me.

My little mans were hungry all now and complaining, they hadn't eaten all morning. I told them pussy holes my children where hungry and they suggested crisps.

I said, 'Nah, my little mans don't eat that shit for breakfast, are you mad? Do you let your children eat that for breakfast?'

They ended up letting us stop at Mc Donald's, that was the best it was getting. I walked in, flanked by three boy dem and my two little mans. Everyone in there was watching us. They must have wondered who the fuck I was with all this boy dem attention. They wouldn't even let me piss in peace.

I had to ask this guy with the way he was going on, 'Come on, do you really think I'm gonna run off and leave my children with you?'

He replied, 'I don't know, but it's better to be safe than sorry.'

I was still playing the covert hypnosis game with them, so I smiled and sat down with my yute mans to eat. I must have looked like a real criminal.

As we drove further and further off the ends, the little mans started to get anxious, wondering where the fuck they were taking us.

Lamar came like my lawyer on the day. He said, 'I hope you know, as my Dad's just helping you with your enquiries, you're taking us back to his car when you've finished.'

The boy dem laughed and agreed.

I'd already let them know I wouldn't be using any Duty Solicitors when I got there. I had a guy already, but I didn't tell them that, so they must have been expecting everything to run smoothly for them.

We finally got there and went through the formalities bullshit, then they locked me up. As soon as we got in that interview room though, everything switched and I was a totally different guy.

One of them even said, 'Aww, Chris, come on now! I thought you was going to cooperate.'

I bet you did, as I gave them pussy holes no comment all the way through. They showed me the one piece of incrimination they took from my house. I laughed, then gave them more no comment.

That was the only piece of info they had that made me uncomfortable and if they wanted me they were going to have to work.

They soon realized that. They wrapped up the interview and sent me back to the cell.

As I got back to the cell, I thought back to all that had happened in my life to bring me to where I was now and I wondered where it was all going to end.

Part 1: AVAILABLE NOW - Part 2: COMING SOON

It's On Top

The Reggie Stepper Story

Reginald Kwame Owusu

LON
DON'S
finest

London's Finest Distribution
London, UK

www.LondonFinestDistribution.com

Info@londonsfinestdistribution.com

Chapter 1

'Babes, I think you're being raided,' my girl said nervously as she came back to the bedroom.

I was high as fuck off cocaine. I had my girl and her lover Sandra in my bed, butt naked. We'd been getting high all night. It didn't sink in straight away. I said, 'Yeah ok, babes.' Then it hit me, *WHAT, RAIDED!* I jumped up as I looked on my table. Cocaine was everywhere. *I'm going jail* as I started hurling shit out of my bedroom window. *Everything seemed to slow down.* BANG, the door came off. SHIT!!! Then I heard what sounded like stampeding elephants running up my stairs. The boy dem got to my bedroom door just as I chucked the last ounce out, but I had the little personal quarter we'd been using in my hand. The first boy dem who got to my room didn't see it. So I had to shove it up my arse, but didn't manage to hide it totally before he screamed, 'FREEZE MOTHER FUCKER, DON'T YOU FUCKING MOVE!'

MP65 in my face. His fellow officers right behind him all screaming, 'FREEZE,' adding more chaos to this already very chaotic situation.

My hands went up in the air slowly. The first boy dem

said, 'Ahh, ahh,' as he covered his eyes, 'put some clothes on, all of you.'

Arse and tits were all out. He didn't see the half wrap of cocaine hanging out my arse because he didn't make me turn round. They stood by the door as I put my tracksuit on and the girls wrapped themselves in towels. There was no opportunity to hide it, so it had to stay up my clenched arse as I walked towards them slowly. One boy dem even asked me, 'Why you walking like that?'

I said, 'I'm just in shock,' as I shook my head.

They took us into my front room and sat us down as they searched through my shit. They were looking for drugs that time, *someone must have ratted me out,* but the boy dem were pissed cos they couldn't find any.

I was calm with the thought that it was all gone, except for the bit hanging out my arse, *I could claim as personal if they found*.

The good thing was, as they searched my yard the Sergeant had asked, 'Have you searched him?'

The one that got to my room first said, 'I saw him butt naked Sarge, he ain't got nothing on him.'

The Police women who were part of the raid were all over me. It seemed like they were turned on by me having two girls butt naked in my bed.

They asked the girls, 'Do you live here with him?'

The girls said, 'No!'

One of the Police women said, 'Oh, that's probably why there isn't much food in the fridge.'

This pissed my girl right off so she said, 'There's no food in this fridge because he eats at ours; now can you hurry up and finish what you're doing so we can get back to sucking his cock.' The Police women didn't like that but I was more thinking, *shut the fuck up, cos they might wonder where you live*. As their search began to seem a little desperate, not having any luck with drugs, they turned their attention to a few of my Ashanti weapon ornaments. *They hadn't found the machines so it was alright.* 'What's this then?' one of them asked holding one of my knives.

'That's just a souvenir officer,' I said, 'but DON'T touch the tip on that arrow!' I shouted as another one almost killed himself. He had my poison tip arrow, tipped with poison from the Golden Dart Frog in his hand, about to see how sharp it was. *There is no known cure for that poison.*

After that the officers calmed down. They could see now that I was alright. *I had even offered to make them all cups of tea.* I was relaxed because I had forgotten that wrap of cocaine. But now it had fallen out my arse and was only a inch away from falling onto the floor in front of all these boy dem. *It was a little bulge in my track suit, caught by my ankle.* I kept my cool though and went through the motions, while I waited for the police to finish up their search.

'Look we've found this, so we're gonna have to nick ya!' (arrest me). They said as I looked at them wondering what it was they had found. *It was a little fucking eighth I had totally forgotten about, pissed!* They hand cuffed me and put me in the meat wagon (police van) as the girls screamed, *'LEAVE HIM, HE HASN'T DONE ANYTHING, WHERE ARE YOU TAKING HIM?'*

To which the police replied, 'He'll be alright, don't worry.' As we travelled to the police station, I was locked away in the back cage like an animal, so I took the opportunity to plug that bit from my ankle up my arse properly. At least I didn't have to worry about that again.

It was straight forward in the police station.

The arresting Sergeant said, 'If you continue to be as polite as you've been all morning, you're gonna go to court and the Judge is going to give you a fine and a slap on the wrist.' *I was out by the afternoon.*

It was cold as I rang my girl while I walked towards Gants Hill train station. I told her, 'I'm out now babes, come pick me up.' About 15 minutes later I saw them driving up the road towards me in my car, looking all fresh and summery; with a bottle of Bacardi. *They had carried on fucking after my arrest, I could see it in their eyes.* I didn't feel like going straight home, so we went back to Sandra's place and carried on fucking there.

That's all I did back then, sell drugs, fix broken machines and fuck!

Life is Good

Chapter 2

I think its best I start at the beginning; you might be getting the wrong impression of me. I was born in 1972 in Thorpe Coombe Hospital off Forest Road in Walthamstow, East London. It was a cold winter my Mum said and she thought, that was the first year the system started to notice that black people were ripe for a new form of exploitation. *My Mum and Dad like so many others were such hard workers.* I had to go to my Nannys house all the time. Where she taught me the English culture. A lovely white lady she was called Aunt Iris. My parents were red blooded Africans, so all they were ever going to teach me, with regards to culture was my original African roots.

I remember as a youngster taking a trip to my Dad's home town in Ghana for the first time. *The climate felt like home and I loved it.* While we were there we went to pay our respects to the local King. As we went into his house, his maids directed us to the back garden where the King was sitting by a lake taking in the scenery. He had one of his grounds men throwing chunks of hard dough bread into the lake. At the age of 4 I wondered what he was feeding until out came the snout of a seven or so foot crocodile. When I saw it I remember *standing there, trembling in fear*.

The King saw I was afraid and told me, 'DO NOT BE SCARED, go over there and look in that bucket.'

In this bucket was a whole heap of baby crocs with bits of hard dough bread amongst them.

The King then explained, 'From the egg these baby crocs are fed bread and nothing else.'

This means they never got a taste for blood; not even fresh water cat fish blood and that made it safe for locals to interact and even swim with them in the local lakes.

The King then went on to explain that, 'This science has been around since the birth of man, where even lions and tigers can be trained to eat just fruit.'

On that same trip we also went to see my Dad's uncle; my great uncle who was the local witch doctor. So although I was born in England, my parents made sure from early that I was going to be well versed in my Ghanaian culture. My Mum even made me learn our native tongue.

I had two older sisters who used to dote on me. We had to share the same bed, all 3 of us and they would fart smelly ones on me all the time and giggle. Although I didn't mean to, I used to wet the bed, so it was like pay back and all part of our bonding.

My Mum really was the centre of all our worlds back then and if she didn't like you or you upset her for whatever reason, she would make you know about it, whether it took a day, weeks or months. Your life wouldn't be comfortable until that beef was cooked and this went for everyone including my Dad.

On one occasion I remember an argument my parents were having. My Mum shouted at my Dad calling him, 'MAD AS SHIT!'

My Dad very rarely swore so for my Mum to say something like that totally surprised and offended him. My Dad refused to talk to my Mum after that for a good 2 weeks. The rest of us in the family thought it was actually a really good nick name for him though.

When my Dad's brothers rang, they would ask my Mum, 'Where's mad as shit?'

That pissed my Dad right off. Until my Dad put his foot down and told everyone he wouldn't be having that any more.

On the rare occasions when my Mum would get physical, she would attack with plates, dashing them wildly. Me, my brothers and sisters kind of learnt to know when she was in the zone and always managed to duck at the right time. She was a damn good shot and more often than not, she caught my Dad square in his face. I sometimes felt sorry for him because of the way the mash potato and gravy would stick to his glasses. It was comical. Me and my brothers used to joke, he needed a little set of wind screen wipers on his glasses to clear the mess so he could see, but it was safe to say that out of the 2 of them my Mum was more cool and down to earth. My Dad to his credit wasn't as judgemental.

In junior school, Winns Primary, I was a very hyper active kid. One of my earliest memories in school was me accidently breaking my friends arm ramping (messing about) with him when I shouldn't have been. My Mum and the teachers were constantly telling me to stop, but I just couldn't sit still for love nor money. I owe a lot to these character building junior school days, playing in that playground. I learnt the meaning of loyalty, feelings of rejection, team work and that an enemy came in all shapes and sizes.

I have to take time to pay respects to Mr Smith who always told me to calm down and redirect that temper. He saw the fire in me from then, but he also saw the good.

It surprised me to hear this white man say, 'If you don't calm down, the world will forget you.'

These home truths rang clear in my head because my

Mum and Dad would tell me the same thing. *Call it sods law and it shouldn't have been the case, but I listened more when the white man said it.*

MUM

Chapter 3

Even as a youngster I did clock (notice) even though I didn't feel the racism that much personally, that some of the teachers didn't like us blacks and any opportunity they got we were called naughty and sent straight to the troublesome class. The thing is, the white yutes were doing exactly the same thing and getting no punishment, but they would leave the black yutes to rot. I guess this is why we must remember, the school system wasn't designed for black people, there was a time when black people weren't even allowed to read. When you think about it, where did all those skin heads and NF go when they grew their hair. Did they just stop being racist, I don't think so. Other tell-tale signs would include when a white pupil made a racist joke and everyone laughed. The racist teachers would laugh too. The golly wog on jam jars was a big joke and the monkey on PG tip was another one. *All those adverts were directed at us. I didn't call it racism then but I'm calling it racism now*. I was alright though, probably because Aunt Iris had taught me cockney, so I ended up high in the pecking order. This meant that the cool girls went out with the little men like me.

I remember Nicky Burns was perfect for me back then and by the bike sheds, I had my first kiss. It was surreal. My lips on hers for longer than the good night peck I got from my Mum. I'll never forget kissing her as hard as I could without tongues and when I tasted her mouth I stopped to spit. *You never forget your first kiss.*

Being one of the cool kids and well-loved both at school and at home, my class mates always wanted me around for all the school events, but at the same time my Mum was very protective of me.

There was a school trip coming up around the time that I wanted to go to, but I didn't think my Mum was going to let me. When I asked her if I could go to the Isle of Wight for a week; I was surprised my Mum said yes without hesitation.

I guess she understood that I was growing up and needed to start learning about independence.

It was the first time I had ever travelled without my parents and I remember the places we visited in Isle of Wight were amazing, both visually and historically. We went to the famous Needle Cliff beaches, the Smugglers Museum and Osborn House where Queen Victoria lived. I loved the place. *Trips like this, I was very lucky to go on* because it was helping mould me at that young age into the character I was going to be.

All in all those junior school days were lovely. *I had a great time*. Being loud and hyperactive got me into a little trouble from time to time at school. I wasn't naughty, but they called me disruptive. At home I rarely got into trouble. I only remember the time me and my cousin Eddie got caught talking about girls. I always used to make up stories that consisted of me linking a blonde haired, blue eyed shorty that seemed to always wear a white t-shirt and tight blue jeans. It was a straight fantasy I'd tell my cousin; until the day his Mum overheard us talking and told my Mum, then I had to have one of those embarrassing birds and the bee's talks. To top that off, I nearly died of more embarrassment when I had to admit to my cousin that I had made it up and none of it was true.

He dropped the shocker on me when he told me, 'All the time you used to say it, I knew it weren't true.'

The embarrassment I felt as a kid was even worse than my Mum giving me the bird's and the bee's talk so I asked, 'Why did you entertain me for so long?'

He replied, 'I loved it.' Needless to say I carried on telling my stories but after that, we always checked our environment before we talked about it.

After a while, in the playground for a joke, some of my school friends started calling me a coconut cause my first kiss was with a white girl and my stories of childhood fantasy always consisted of a blonde chick with blue eyes and tight blue jeans. I also had a love for princes paste and shepherd's pie; as well as obviously my yam and plantain, but they never saw me eat that because that was what I ate at home. *My mates didn't know what they were talking about.* I was more cultured than them, but it's true they didn't know. Even though they called me a coconut playing around, no one troubled me. I wasn't really ever a victim of racism in school either, even though if they were being racist to one, they are being racist to all because united we stood and divided we always fall.

One of my closest friends Eric D was a gypsy and he would teach me about his culture too. To be fair, I did talk like a cockney probably because of Aunt Iris, but that made me alright with the mods and the skin heads. At this point in time, it was their time to rule and the streets of London were openly racist. The police would turn a blind eye to their atrocities because they probably held the same views as the skin heads. I saw them fuck the Asians up on a regular. They kicked, punched and spat at them all the time and

I could tell that if they ever got the opportunity to kill any of them, the hate was so real they would have.

My Mum must have felt like because that happened to them, we should move. My parents probably worked so hard so they could and the time finally came when my parents had made enough money to move out of Priory Court. Personally I didn't want to leave Priory Court even though it was a little rough. I knew everyone there so I was alright. I was young so even though we were only moving down the road, it seemed like miles away.

We moved into a house on Lyne Crescent. I was about 10 at the time and after we moved, my other little cousins Ranks and Star who I spent a lot of these early days playing with moved away too.

My life took a turn and now consisted of my BMX bike, birthday parties and body popping.

OUT NOW

THE KINGS PEACE TREATY

I WILL NEVERPUT NO EUROPEON GEOGRAPHICAL LANDMARK BEFORE MY BROTHER.

WHEN ANYONE COMES AS A STRANGER FROM A NEIGHBOURING AREA I WILL EMBRACE HIM AND TREAT HIM LIKE A KING.

I WILL NOT GO IN ANYMANS AREA AND PROMOTE VIOLENCE IN PROTEST TO PROMOTE MY AREA.

WHEN I SEE A BLACK MAN ON THE STREET I WILL HAIL AND ACKNOWLEDGE HIM IN RESPECT OF THE SUFFERING WE AND OUR ANCESTORS HAVE FACED FOR CENTURIES.

I WILL LOOK AT NO BLACK MAN AS LESS THAN A KING.

I WILL LOOK AT NO BLACK WOMAN AS LESS THAN A QUEEN, BECAUSE THE BLACK WOMBMAN IS THE MOTHER OF ALL CIVILIASATION AND WE MUST PROTECT HER.

I WILL LINK UP WITH EVERYMAN FROM EVERY ENDS TO BUILD MY PEOPLE AND TO BUILD A BETTER EARTH FOR OUR FUTURE GENERATIONS.

Written by
Yisrael Immanuel
@TheKingsPeaceTreaty

Similar Genre and Associate Authors

Chris Sibia: A Product of My Environment Part 2 – COMING SOON
Reginald Owusu: It's On Top The Reggie Stepper Story Part 1
Burnie Brightly: In The Beginning
Von Mozar: Ignorance Kills
Von Mozar: Sexfiend
Von Mozar: Little Jamaica
Von Mozar: Mr Bling
Von Mozar: On The Endz – OUT: 14/2/2018
Levi P.S: Through My Eyes (The Spirit Of A Prince)
Robyn Travis: Mama Can't Raise No Man
Robyn Travis: Prisoner to the Streets
Sherlock: Different, Different Part 2
Jonathan Buffong & Brenda Downes: Warriors of the Cage
Davis J. Williams: And Along Came A Lion
Davis J. Williams: No Enemy Within
Jasmine Johnson: Mr Soon Come
Chrisitian Niova Diawara Small: Wake up and smell the Fufu
Courttia Newland: The Scholar (A West Side Story)
Claudine Duberry BA, MA: Guns, Gangs and the Implication for Social Workers
Jaja Soze: Street Boys
Stephen Graham: I'm A Gun
Ted Pitman: The Monkey Bars of Life
Pearson Nurse: My Journey through Racism
Bernie Grant MP: Dawn to Dusk

Further Education

AFRICAN HISTORY

Llaila O Afrika: African Holistic Health

Llaila O Afrika: Melanin

Robin Walker: When We Ruled

Ivan Van Sertima: They Came Before Columbus

David Muhammad: Black Studies

Chancellor Williams: The Destruction of Black Civilization

CC Blackman: Towards the Destruction of a Nigger Mentality

Robin Walker: Blacks and Religion (Volume One)

Walter Rodney: How Europe Underdeveloped Africa

GOOD BOOKS

Jose Silva: The Silva Mind Control Method

David Morehouse: Remote Viewing

Charles Arthur: The Art of Passing the Buck

Richard Edwards & Nigel Stockwell: Trusts and Equity

Robert Kiyosaki: Rich Dad Poor Dad

Nathalie Nahai: Webs of Influence

Malcolm Gladwell: The Tipping Point

Organisations Helping the Community

LED Talks

www.AccessUk.org

www.GangsUnite.org

www.Ukblack-links.com

www.Jimmyasherfoundation.org

Wipers

www.Mentivity.com

www.Inspiredfutures.com

www.Reachsociety.com

www.Father2father.com

www.Robertlevyfoundation.org

www.Communitiesfirst.uk.com

www.Afreshstartct.org

Family Circle Consultancy